T0304863

MILITARY MINDSET

About the Author

Ant Middleton is the author of three *Sunday Times* No. 1 best-sellers, *First Man In*, *The Fear Bubble* and *Zero Negativity*. His books have sold over two million copies around the world. He is an adventurer, public speaker and television presenter, best known as the front man for Channel 4's hit show *SAS: Who Dares Wins*.

MILITARY MINDSET

LESSONS FROM THE BATTLEFIELD

Ant Middleton

Written with Tim Andrews

HODDER &
STOUGHTON

First published in Great Britain in 2024 by Hodder & Stoughton Limited
An Hachette UK company

1

Copyright © Ant Middleton 2024

The right of Anthony Middleton to be identified as the Author of the Work has been
asserted by him in accordance with the Copyright, Designs and Patents Act 1988.

A CIP catalogue record for this title is available from the British Library

Hardback ISBN 9781399737005
Trade Paperback ISBN 9781399737012

Typeset in Celeste by Hewer Text UK LTD, Edinburgh
Printed and bound in Great Britain by Clays Ltd, Elcograf S.p.A.

Hodder & Stoughton policy is to use papers that are natural, renewable
and recyclable products and made from wood grown in sustainable
forests. The logging and manufacturing processes are expected to
conform to the environmental regulations of the country of origin.

Hodder & Stoughton Limited
Carmelite House
50 Victoria Embankment
London EC4Y 0DZ

www.hodder.co.uk

CONTENTS

'In war it is less profitable to win many battles and learn little than to win one battle and learn much.'

General Vo Nguyen Giap

'The more you sweat in peace, the less you bleed in war.'

General Norman Schwarzkopf, US Army

INTRODUCTION
THE MAKING OF AN ELITE MINDSET

The battlefield is the most unforgiving environment on the planet. A single mistake or a split-second moment of indecision can mean the difference between life and death. Between victory and defeat.

Being in the military means volunteering for hazardous service. You're going to find yourself in some very difficult situations, against hostile forces, and there's a good chance you'll be exposed to some unpleasant stuff. You'll likely witness or experience things that would distress the average person.

That's why the military is the toughest and most demanding career. You need to be seriously hardened before you go into the combat zone. You need to learn how to deal with shock. How to control your emotions. How to suck it up and get on with the job, even when you've just been exposed to something truly horrid.

If you're not prepared – if you've not been pushed to your limits physically, mentally and emotionally – it could cost you your life, or the lives of your friends.

Some of my most valuable learning experiences came at the sharp end of conflict. Many of those lessons still apply to my life today, whether I'm climbing K2 or Mount Everest or embarking on a new challenge.

The military is where I learned how to push through the pain barrier. How to deal with hardship and deprivation. How to be consistent in my discipline and process fear. How to lead. In 9 Parachute Squadron, Royal Engineers, the Royal Marines and later in the dog-eat-dog world of Special Forces, I became the very best version of myself. The best soldier possible.

During my time in the military, the battlefield became my training ground. Across multiple tours, in some of the most hostile places in the world, I lived and breathed soldiering. I was totally focused on my goals. And I was continually being pushed.

What helped me survive was my mindset. I felt invincible. Almost as if I had a shield around me. The way I saw it, if I had been shot or killed it would have been an insult to my skills as an operator. I had an air of arrogance, but this was partly a defence mechanism. A way of bullet-proofing my mind. If I went into battle thinking I was the best and I couldn't get killed, and then someone shot me in the head, I wouldn't know about it. Because I'd be dead. But at least I would go out thinking I was the best.

Your mindset will get you through the toughest moments in your life. That is the one thing no one else can take from you. Your mindset is entirely yours, so why give it up? You can be locked up in prison, or your legs might get blown off by an Improvised Explosive Device (IED), but no one should ever be able to take away your mindset, because that is really all you have.

An impenetrable mindset is the ultimate weapon. But you can only gain that mentality by staying completely true to yourself – and that is far from easy. Because the more you try to stay true to yourself, the more outside forces will try to cut you down. The onslaught feels unendurable. Never-ending. It's tempting to veer away from your true self, to put your head back below the parapet. Get back into your box. But when you do that, you'll be living a lie. And you'll have to fight very hard to work your way back to your true self.

The secret is to trust in who you are. In order to do that you have to know who you are, and to know who you are you've got to put yourself through the mill physically, psychologically and emotionally.

The more you do that, the more you expose yourself to hardship and new challenges, the more you'll learn about yourself. And when you repeat that process, constantly, you're going to take off more layers – and you'll get closer to discovering your true self. You'll find your centre. Once you've got that, you'll realise what you are capable of.

You'll gain the military mindset.

Although this is a book about war and what it taught me, these lessons are relevant to everyday life – to the life you're living right now. The military mindset will help to give you a greater knowledge and awareness of physical, mental and emotional resilience and open your eyes to what you can achieve if you're prepared to learn about yourself.

That equally applies to the battles and generals of history. Whether it's Alexander the Great demonstrating leadership in the searing heat of the Gedrosian desert or the inspiring example of the Glosters' last stand at the Battle of the Imjin River in the Korean War, there are vital lessons that can help anyone navigate life's toughest moments. And the great thing about *Military Mindset* is that you don't need to read it chronologically to gain that knowledge. You can dip in and out whenever you need positive reinforcement and jump straight to the lesson that relates to you. Each lesson or example is short enough to read or listen to on your daily commute, or during a session on the treadmill.

Whatever your circumstances – whether you're thinking about a change in career but are afraid to commit to that first step, or you're going through difficulties in your personal life – you'll find something here for you.

PART ONE

TRAINING

DON'T GET CARRIED AWAY WITH THE DESTINATION

When people begin a task, or set a challenge for themselves, they often fall into the trap of focusing too hard on the destination, to the detriment of almost everything else.

The problem with this approach is that when they fall short, which happens all the time in life, they become consumed by their failure to reach that objective, whether that means landing a contract or winning a sports competition. They lose sight of how much they've already accomplished on the journey. They look at what they *haven't* achieved – when they should be looking at what they *have*. They define themselves by their failure to reach their destination.

At root level, failure is a man-made construct. It's something you're told by other people, when in reality only you know how you feel. Yes, you might have technically failed in the eyes of someone else. But as long as you don't personally *feel* like a failure, as long as you keep learning and growing, striving to become a better version of who you are, then you're never truly failing.

The key to understanding this is to take that destination and put it to the back of your mind. Don't look towards your ultimate objective, otherwise you're going to get overwhelmed by the scale of the challenge in front of you. Instead, break down your goals into *phases of commitment*. Ask yourself, 'What am I going to learn from this commitment along the way? What lessons will I absorb? What will I find out about myself?'

Apply this mindset and you'll have a much better chance of doing whatever it is you're aiming to do. You'll start to understand that when the challenge scares you, when you feel like running away from it – that's when you need to dive in. Your body is priming itself for the challenge lying ahead of it. Tell yourself, 'I'm going to really commit to this first phase,' and you're less likely to give in to those feelings.

This is exactly how I approached Selection.

The failure rate on Selection is very high. That can overwhelm some people. When you look at the overall effort required, it's easy to feel intimidated.

I never looked further ahead than each separate phase of commitment. When I began the first phase, I viewed it as a tremendous learning experience. I approached it thinking to myself, 'I'm going to learn a lot of stuff during this stage. I'm going to find out about my physical capabilities, my inner strength, and how far I can push the limits of my body and mind. If I survive this phase, it'll be a massive personal achievement. Even if I don't make it through the next phase, I'll have ticked off one stage of commitment. I'll go back to my unit knowing I've got the first stage in the bag, and I can still have another stab at Selection.'

When I made it through, the second stage became my next focus of commitment. In my head, I knew that if I passed that meant I would be a very good soldier. I'd know how to operate in a very demanding environment, and even if I didn't pass the next stage of Selection, I would have still learned a massive amount about my qualities as a soldier. I could go back to my unit with my head held high, knowing that I'd passed the two stages. Yes, going back to do Selection again is a daunting prospect – but it's also an opportunity.

A lot of the guys didn't look at Selection this way, however. They'd make it through the first phase, but then they'd fail at the second stage, or they'd crack during a later stage. At which point they would return to their units and tell their mates, 'I didn't make it. I failed Selection.'

Actually, that's the wrong way of looking at it. They're ignoring what they've achieved along the way. I take my hat off to anyone who has survived the first phase of Selection, because it is brutal.

The guys who considered themselves failures weren't thinking about what they had achieved already, or what they could learn from their experience. They were thinking only about the entirety, the end goal.

Ultimately, that can stop people from committing to action. The challenge becomes too overwhelming, the destination appears too far away and the possibility of failing to reach it is too big. The odds aren't in their favour, so they don't commit at all.

But when you break down a big goal into smaller stages of commitment, you start to look at it differently. You'll begin to accept the possibility of failure along the way – and more importantly, you'll learn from those failures, turning them to your advantage.

Learning is crucial to understanding the difference between journey and destination.

We're often told nowadays, 'It's okay to fail.' But that's only true if you absorb the lessons from the original failure – if you analyse why it didn't work out, so you can regroup, go again and tackle it differently the next time.

If you continue to repeatedly fail, you're not learning from it. Instead, face the task by thinking, 'I'm going to learn from this phase of commitment no matter what.' When you attempt it again, you'll see what you're truly capable of. You'll start to tell yourself, 'Yes, I am capable', and those words will be backed up by action.

You'll no longer view things in crude terms of failure and success. It becomes about the *learning journey*. Taking what you learn from each loss into the next game, or the next project or mission.

Flipping those losses into wins.

Of course, this won't be a perfectly smooth process. You're going to continue to lose some of the time. But learning from your losses is as important as breaking down the challenge into phases of commitment.

Military operations are in some respects high-stakes learning experiences. All soldiers are going to fail a mission at some point. It then becomes about asking yourself, 'What did we learn from that attack? How can we do things differently next time? What's the lesson here?' That allows you to reorganise and attack again.

IF YOU'RE NOT LEARNING FROM YOUR LOSSES, YOU'RE DESTINED TO REPEAT THE SAME MISTAKES INSTEAD OF TURNING THEM TO YOUR ADVANTAGE.

World War I shows what happens when you don't learn from failure. The generals on the Western Front kept throwing men at the problem of how to break the quagmire of trench warfare, expecting a different result using the same means. They didn't learn their lessons. They kept using the same approach, blindly hoping for a better outcome, at the cost of millions of lives.

If you're not learning from your losses, you're destined to repeat the same mistakes instead of turning them to your advantage. Because how do you expect to win if you haven't learned how to *lose*?

The easiest thing to do in life is to step back from a commitment. To say to yourself, 'I'm not going to play this game, because I might lose.' A lot of people do this. They become so petrified of losing – and therefore being defined by that feeling – that they go through their lives without committing to anything that will take them outside their comfort zone. They're unable to face jeopardy, or deal with setbacks. They stay in their safe spaces.

It takes courage to keep playing the game: to accept the constant presence of failure, and the commitment to fail, in your daily life. Harder, yes. But that mindset is also much more rewarding. It's the gateway drug to success.

Once you commit to failure, the more you play the game, the more you will learn about the game, and therefore about life and yourself. And the more games you're going to win. You'll be a step nearer to where you want to be. That destination will seem a little closer.

There are only upsides to committing to failure. With that commitment will come self-belief. That's a gift only you can give yourself. Other people might tell you that they believe in you, but those are just empty words. That belief has to come from within you, and you get that through committing to action, by stepping into new spaces all the time and learning from those experiences.

Every time you step into a new space, you're entering somewhere you've never been before. And you're going to learn something, regardless of the outcome. That will help you grow as a person. Even if it's just a tiny percentage, you'll still be a better, more experienced person than you were before you had committed to that action. To that failure.

In truth, there's only one destination in life that matters: the big one that is coming to all of us eventually. Everything else is just part of the journey. And whatever path we choose, it's going to be littered with failures. You can't change that. But you can control whether you learn from them or not. Failure presents an opportunity. It gives you the chance to reassess your goals and think about what you want to achieve in life.

If you're embarking on a new challenge in life, such as a change of career, don't let the scale of the task stop you from taking the plunge. Instead of obsessing about the eventual goal, focus on the separate phases of commitment you'll need to move through before you get there. Apply yourself wholly to each stage of your journey. Face up to failure and learn from your experiences, and you'll be amazed at what you can achieve.

LESSON 2

SET ACHIEVABLE GOALS

Goals are the milestones on the road to your destination. Whether that's a dream you want to realise, the person you want to become, or a mission you're trying to complete – they are the things you should be really passionate about.

We're constantly being told to write our goals down, as if that is somehow going to help us achieve them. That's nonsense. You shouldn't have to write down your goals. If you really want to achieve something, it should already be there in your head. It should dominate your thoughts daily. If you need to write it down on a piece of paper, frankly, you're not going to be passionate about it.

Whatever your goal may be, the key to achieving it is always the same: *break it down.*

People constantly make the mistake of setting themselves huge goals. As soon as they do that, they make their goals almost unachievable. The task in front of them becomes too overwhelming, the distance too great. So they give up before they've even started.

Goals should be tiny. Don't bite off too big a chunk because you're immediately setting yourself up for failure. If you break down your goals, you're making them achievable. And you're also going to get to where you want to be a lot quicker.

A military mission is essentially a series of goals the team has to navigate together. The first goal might be something as simple as getting to the target. Once you're there that's your first goal completed. You think to yourself, 'Great, I'm here now. I'm on target.' Your sense of achievement heightens.

Then the second goal could be something like clearing the buildings within the compound. In my head, I'll tackle each building as a separate goal. 'Building two, clear,' I'll think. 'Good, that's another green tick in the box.'

Another operator might break down their goals differently. They might treat each room clearance as an individual goal. But that's the great thing about goals. You can break them down however you want – however it works for you. The only rule is: *Don't make them too big.*

The next goal then becomes making my way to the rendezvous point (RV). We've completed the mission. The goal now is extraction. Again, you don't have to treat this as a single goal. You might decide to turn each kilometre to the RV into a separate goal. The main thing is that you're setting yourself small – and therefore manageable – goals.

They become *small victories.*

That's what goals should be, in your life. Small victories that contribute to the overall bigger victory.

This system doesn't just apply to the military. You can use it for almost any goal in life, whether it's working on your physical fitness, or setting goals for your team in the workplace.

Suppose you want to lose weight. Don't tell yourself, 'I need to lose twenty kilos.' You're making the goal far too big. Instead make your goal losing two kilos in the first few weeks or month. Take it from there.

Whatever you're aiming for, it's about earning those small victories, which in turn will make you see what you're capable of. That capability will turn into self-belief, and the self-belief you've acquired will carry you through to the next goal.

Goals also have to be sustainable. It's no good setting yourself a new goal every two or three months. If you do that, all the energy and enthusiasm you've earned from your previous achievements will disappear. It won't last long enough to carry you through.

Instead, make your goals a daily part of your life. Weave them into every aspect of your day. Getting up and going to the gym, for example: that's a goal. Tick that one off. How good does that make you feel? You're one step closer to being where you want to be physically and mentally. Then you're in a position where you can use the positivity that you've gained from that small victory to pursue the next goal.

The next small victory.

Once you start being present in the moment, you'll be able to focus more fully on your immediate goal. In my younger days in the military, I never dreamed of being in the SF. That wasn't a destination for me until much later on in my career.

When I joined the Royal Marines, my mindset was very much: *take each week as it comes*. I didn't allow myself to look any further ahead than that. But as the weeks passed, I realised that I was one of the fittest guys in the group. I was more switched-on and disciplined than most of the other blokes. So I made my next goal to get a PT Superior. This is an award you get midway through training, given to candidates who perform outstandingly in the gym phase. That involved a few weeks of hard work, finding out more about myself, that I loved what I did.

I came top of the pass-out parade and got my PT Superior, which prepared me for the next stage of training. At this stage the instructors introduced weight into the equation. We had to complete various exercises wearing full kit, webbing and daysack, and eventually our Bergens and weapons. Exercises included carry drills, casualty evacuation (CASEVAC) drills, rope work, with the final one being the all-singing, all-dancing live-firing drill.

So my next goals became to finish top in map-reading and my live-firing. After that, I made getting my green beret my next goal. Then I targeted the reconnaissance course, then the sniper course. Once I'd done that, I set myself the target of making Lance Corporal. Getting a tour of duty in Afghanistan under my belt.

At every step of the process, I was breaking down those goals in a way that worked for me.

This mindset worked for me in Afghanistan as well. Every patrol we went on, every corner we turned became a separate goal. We'd get through the morning without getting into contact with the enemy, and I'd count that as a goal.

If you keep on setting yourself large goals, if the goal is too far away or it takes too long to get there, you're probably going to get bored, distracted or side-tracked by something else during the journey. You're closing your mind to the opportunities that might unexpectedly come your way from the periphery.

Don't ignore these opportunities. Yes, they might divert you from your goal, but in a *positive way*. They might enhance you as an individual, give you the chance to grow. Then, once you've explored this opportunity coming in from the side, this *positive detour*, you can direct your attention back to the overall goal that you have set yourself.

Don't allow yourself to get too fixated on your larger ambitions. It's fine – healthy, in fact – to have them in your life, as long as they're realistic and you're not indulging in self-delusion. But don't focus on those goals to the exclusion of everything else in your life. Don't lose sight of the ground in front of you.

Starting a new job can often be an overwhelming experience. Make the process more manageable by setting small goals for yourself initially. Take each week as it comes, work hard and you'll gain confidence and self-belief from each small victory you achieve along the way.

SEIZE THE OPPORTUNITY TO IMPROVE

There are no short-cuts to passing Selection. To become part of the SF brotherhood, you need absolute dedication to being the very best version of yourself.

The historian Josephus, writing in the first century AD, said the Roman army made their drills 'bloodless battles' so that when it came to the actual fighting their battles would be like 'bloody drills'. Our training has the same objective.

We make it as close to the real thing as it's possible to get. It's brutal and often very dangerous, sometimes even life-threatening. But we're prepared to work. We're always looking to put in more effort, even if it only increases our performance by one or two per cent. On the battlefield those tiny percentage points can mean the difference between success and failure.

Those percentage points are crucial in your everyday life. If you can improve your work, your mindset, your energy by even one or two per cent, you will be on the right path. You have to be relentless in your self-improvement. Improving by

one or two per cent might seem insignificant in the beginning. But when repeated over a long time, these changes
become massive. And if there's a choice to better yourself, it
doesn't matter how exhausted you are – you should always
say yes.

Improvement is impossible without humility and honesty.
Be humble enough to accept criticism. Be honest with yourself. To know when your standard isn't good enough. And
work to improve, *every single day.*

That was always my mindset. I might have spent some time
on patrol, for example, and when my shift ended, instead of
switching off, I'd think, 'Well, I'm up and about, might as well
go through the mission briefing again.' I did this without hesi-
tation – because I was absolutely motivated to improve myself
at every opportunity.

When the opportunity to improve is offered to you – pounce
on it. Always say yes. Believe me, you'll never regret it.

Continuous self-improvement is critical to personal and
professional growth. At work, look to expand your skillsets
by volunteering for the things no one else wants to do and
applying for training courses. Even if it's not directly related
to your role, the sense of improvement you will feel from
being in a new space will translate to your daily work.

IMPROVEMENT IS IMPOSSIBLE WITHOUT HUMILITY AND HONESTY. BE HUMBLE ENOUGH TO ACCEPT CRITICISM. BE HONEST WITH YOURSELF. TO KNOW WHEN YOUR STANDARD ISN'T GOOD ENOUGH. AND WORK TO IMPROVE, *EVERY SINGLE DAY.*

LESSON 4

BE CONSISTENT IN YOUR DISCIPLINE

Discipline, at the most basic level, is about doing the things you don't want to do, but you know you need to do.

That normally means doing the small things. Discipline isn't necessary for the big things in life. You should be motivated to do the big things anyway. Discipline is about paying attention to the details, no matter how small or seemingly insignificant.

The military places a premium on personal discipline. It's one of the very first lessons you learn when you join.

For example, we had to look immaculate in our ceremonial uniform – our No. 1s. They weren't bothered about checking whether our boots had been buffed or our cap badges were looking smart, because they could see all of this stuff. It was on the surface. They were interested in the other stuff. The things they *couldn't* see.

Cotter pins are used to attach your badge to your ceremonial cap. There's a brass backing plate that goes on the reverse of the cap badge to hold it in place. You lift your collar up, put on the badge using the holes in the plate, making sure the badge is flush against it. Then you push the pin through, securing both plate and cap badge, and fold your collar back down.

No one can see the pin: it's hidden behind the badge and plate. But that pin still had to be polished with Brasso to within an inch of its life. The plate too. Everything needed to be *immaculate*. You couldn't cut corners, either, because they'd lift up your collar and take the pin out to see if the other side looked bang on. If it wasn't up to scratch, you'd have to run around the parade ground with a heavy artillery shell filled with cement held above your head.

The first time I had to do this I remember thinking, 'Why do I need to Brasso the back of a pin? What does it matter if it's polished or not?' But then I began to realise that's what discipline is all about: dealing with the unseen things *as if they're seen.* Being disciplined enough to realise that the small things count.

If you mess up repeatedly on the small things, because you don't think they're relevant, then trust me: sooner or later you're going to trip up in a big way.

It might not happen for a while, but sooner or later that mindset is going to lead to a catastrophic failure.

I've always enjoyed the disciplined life. The military encourages that mindset. But to do it to the best of your ability, you need to layer your own personal discipline on top.

I'd spend an hour or more buffing my pin before going onto the parade square. A single epaulette might take me a few hours before I felt I was good to go. That was me adding an extra layer of discipline to the task.

I could probably have spent half the time polishing that pin and it would have looked perfectly fine to the casual observer. But if I had done that, I'd have that nagging voice in the back of my head telling me that I could have done better.

I BEGAN TO REALISE THAT'S WHAT DISCIPLINE IS ALL ABOUT: DEALING WITH THE UNSEEN THINGS *AS IF THEY'RE SEEN*. BEING DISCIPLINED ENOUGH TO REALISE THAT THE SMALL THINGS COUNT.

I only really comprehended the importance of this mindset when I went into combat. On the battlefield, small details can make an outsized difference to the outcome. That's why I paid attention to things like oiling my magazines, letting the springs relax between ops. We'd make sure that everyone on the team punched the coordinates into their GPS units, so we all knew where we were going, not just the team leader or the second-in-command (2iC).

If you're not consistently disciplined, that might lead to a fatality on your team, or mission failure.

Maintaining your discipline eradicates doubt. But you need to do the job properly to get to that point. Half measures of discipline aren't good enough. The springs in my magazines might be nicely relaxed, or I might have oiled the clips to a reasonably high standard, but if I stop there and think, 'That'll do. That's good enough,' then I'm going into battle with a chance of something going wrong. Doing the job to eighty or ninety per cent of your ability isn't going to cut it. Even one or two per cent might impact on the mission. Discipline requires giving a hundred per cent of the effort. Only then will you know that you're good to go. Anything less, and you're opening the door to doubt. You're setting yourself up to fail.

The great thing about discipline is that after a while, once you achieve consistency of discipline, it turns into motivation.

Suppose you decide to get fit. You commit yourself to getting up at five o'clock in the morning each day before work to hit the gym for half an hour. What's more, you maintain that discipline for a few months. After a while, you start to see the results both physically and mentally. Your endorphins are flowing, you have more energy, you sleep better, you feel like you're attacking the day.

That discipline then flips into motivation, because the positive changes that you're seeing and feeling will motivate you to get up the next day. You'll hit the gym even on the days you're not really feeling it. You know the results you're gaining from this continued commitment. Then you have a choice to either maintain that discipline or evolve it into something else.

When I came off a mission, I actually loved stripping down and cleaning my weapon, firing off a few tester rounds on the range. Because the whole time I was thinking, 'My weapon didn't fail me on that last op. That's great. I know that if I keep treating this piece of equipment properly, if I keep being disciplined with it, then it won't let me down.'

By treating my weapon properly, I knew it would treat me well in return. That became my motivation: to make sure my weapon wouldn't malfunction. Therefore, I was motivated to stick to that cleaning routine. My reward was to go into battle knowing that I could rely on my primary weapon.

I like to think of motivation as the *enjoyable form of discipline*. It's the reward for the effort you've put in. But you can only get there by being consistent with your discipline.

A lot of people let themselves down because they're not willing to stick with being disciplined for long enough to flip it into motivation. They're not willing to be consistent. They tick along and do just enough. But that won't work. Doing the bare minimum isn't being disciplined.

Discipline is asking yourself, constantly, 'Is this good enough? Have I done enough?' Only you know the answer to that question. Only you know whether you've truly put in the effort or not. That means being honest with yourself. If the answer is, 'No, I could have done more,' then you'll never get to that point where discipline transforms into motivation.

Motivation is a powerful thing. It allows you to aim for goals. But when you hit that goal, complacency might creep in. Then you have to go back to being disciplined again. This is a cycle that happens to all of us, throughout life.

You might be motivated to do the Royal Marine Commando course, for example. So you join the Marines. You're hyper-disciplined and motivated for the entire duration of that eight-month course. At the end of it you're given the green beret. Then the complacency starts to creep in. You start to think that you don't need to maintain that level of discipline now that you've reached your goal.

Then the sniper course comes round. You want to do the course, which means going back to being disciplined. Waking up early, studying your maps, working on your ghillie suit, checking that the camo is correct, that your weapon is zeroed. You've successfully flipped from complacency back into that mode of consistent discipline. Suddenly you're motivated again.

Maintaining your personal discipline will make your life easier in a hundred different ways.

Here's what consistent discipline looks like. For the first four weeks of Selection, I had to cover extreme distances, on a time-sensitive course, navigating by myself, with extreme weight on my back. Each day on that stage, before I went to bed, I'd set my alarm to go off every couple of hours in the night. I'd wake up, drink a litre of water, walk out of the accommodation block, head into the shower block, fill my water bottle, return to my bed, set down the filled-up water bottle next to me. Go back to sleep.

You have to carry a certain amount of weight on Selection, plus food and water, which is entirely down to you. You don't want to be slacking on water on the hills: that's asking for trouble. But a lot of the guys weren't hydrating before they attempted the next course. They'd wake up dehydrated after a good five or six-hours' sleep. Which meant they had to take more water with them in their already heavy Bergens so they could rehydrate along the way. Some lads would be carrying a couple of litres of water on their backs.

Staying disciplined at night meant that I didn't need to carry as much water as the others. Even though it meant having to break my sleep, I felt the payoff was worth it. It's a marginal thing, but it gave me an edge.

Consistency of discipline is a prerequisite for achieving any goal, in any walk of life. Achieve that by following the military mindset. Do the things that you don't want to do but you know you should do. Never make the mistake of thinking that 'just enough' is good enough. Strive to do the basic things to a high standard, *consistently*.

Before long, you'll see that discipline evolves into motivation. Then you've got yourself a *disciplined motivator*. And that is someone who cannot be easily broken.

If you're looking to raise standards in your team, revert back to the basics. Get everyone doing the simple things to a consistently high standard. Re-establish the groundworks of discipline. Motivation will follow.

THE ROMAN LEGION – HISTORY'S MOST DISCIPLINED SOLDIERS

The story of the Roman empire is the story of the triumph of the legions.

Being a Roman soldier meant becoming part of the most disciplined fighting force in the world. Recruits had to undergo four months of basic training, including marches of up to twenty miles a day, learning to swim, ride on horseback, build marching camps, lay roads, dig earthwork and even lay out new towns. Most importantly, they learned how to fight to win.

The recruits practised with wooden swords that weighed twice as much as the real thing to help strengthen their muscles, landing blows on stout timber posts. They trained twice a day, fought mock battles with blunted weapons and trained to soldier in compact formations.

The Romans placed a lot of emphasis on discipline. Punishments could be brutal. Anyone guilty of a minor offence might get flogged or fined. Deserters were put to death. The worst punishment was dished out to units that fled in battle or otherwise brought shame on themselves. They were 'decimated' – all the soldiers from that unit were divided into groups of ten and made to draw straws. The soldier in each group with the shortest lot was then stoned or clubbed to death by his mates. Barbaric, maybe. But effective.

Every aspect of training was designed to harden the men, so that they would be better prepared for battle. It was discipline that allowed the Romans to stay in their formation in the middle of battle, even when the odds were massively stacked against them. Nowhere is this more evident than during the Boudican rebellion.

In AD 43, the Romans had invaded Britain. Although they had crushed opposition across most of the south of the island, the northern and western tribes remained unruly and a potential source of trouble.

In AD 60, the province went up in flames. One of Rome's client kings in Britain, a man called Prasutagus, ruled the Iceni tribe. When he died the Romans annexed the kingdom and set about plundering it. They seized the lands of the local elites and humiliated the royal household. Roman soldiers whipped Prasutagus's wife, Boudica, and raped her daughters.

The Icenians rose up against their Roman occupiers. They were quickly joined by another tribe, called the Trinovantes, who had their own reasons for hating the Romans. At Colchester, St. Alban and London tens of thousands of civilians were slaughtered, mutilated or burned alive.

When the news reached the local governor, Suetonius Paulinus, he had a serious problem. His forces were scattered across the island on garrison duty. The capital had fallen, and there was a good chance the rest of the British tribes might side with the rebels.

Paulinus didn't allow himself to get in a flap. Instead he gathered together his men and sought battle with Boudica and her rebels at the earliest opportunity.

Paulinus settled on a well-defended site approached by a narrow passage, with woods and hills guarding his flanks and rear. In front of the men the gully opened out into a wide plain devoid of broken ground or any kind of cover. Across the plain they faced the rebel force.

The odds didn't look good for Rome. They had roughly 10,000 men. The rebels numbered at least 100,000 and may have been even bigger.

The nature of the ground meant that the rebels were forced to advance on the Romans through the congested defile, robbing them of their numerical advantage. As they advanced, the rebels threw huge numbers of missiles at the Romans, but they maintained their discipline and held their ground, waiting to release their javelins until the enemy was within killing range. In the tight confines of the gully, at close range, the soldiers could hardly miss. The Britons suffered huge casualties.

Paulinus then gave the signal. His men advanced. That must have been a terrifying sight for the rebels, and they tried to run for it, but found their escape route blocked by the baggage train. Many were cut to pieces before they could flee. It's thought that 80,000 rebels were killed in a single day. Whereas the Romans lost about four hundred men. This was a catastrophic defeat for Boudica. The rebellion soon died out. The stubborn discipline of the Roman soldiers in battle had saved the province from disaster.

DON'T LET YOUR MISTAKES WIN

Mistakes are inevitable in life. This commonly occurs when your personal discipline slips or becomes less consistent. Then you easily find yourself slipping into complacency.

When this happens the important thing is to stop that seed of doubt from taking over. Don't let it grow. Self-doubt is a disease. Your mind can become loud and overcrowded with negative thoughts. It can put you in a spiral and a sense of doom can take over. When this happens, it's important to not let your focus slip because you've screwed up – which we all do anyway, all of the time, because we're human. Instead, use it as an opportunity to learn.

Your mistakes don't define you, so don't let them win. Whenever you start slipping into complacency, use that as a motivation. Look at it as a springboard to allow you to go back to being disciplined in your habits.

Everyone screws up at work. When it happens to you, don't let it dominate your outlook. Learn your lesson, dust yourself down and go again.

'The sages do not consider that making no mistakes is a blessing. They believe, rather, that the great virtue of man lies in his ability to correct his mistakes and continually to make a new man of himself.'

Wang Yangming, Chinese general, philosopher and politician (1472–1529)

LESSON 6

PUSH THROUGH THE PAIN

Pain is a daily part of life in the military. We're exposed to it in a way that the vast majority of people will never experience.

I'm not talking about involuntary pain – illness or accidents, the things we can't avoid. What I mean is *voluntary pain*. Pain that you have chosen to submit to as part of the process of attaining a specific goal or objective.

When you're being thrashed on in training, and you've got a heavy Bergen on your back, weighing anything up to one hundred and twenty pounds, and every cell in your body is screaming at you to stop walking, when you feel like you can't take another step – that's voluntary pain.

In those situations, you have to first of all realise that the voice telling you to stop isn't in your mind. It's your *body*.

Our brains are biologically hardwired to prepare us for the worst. When you're experiencing extreme pain, that's your body's early-warning system kicking in. Telling you that if you go on any further, something really bad is going to happen. It's going to result in a life-threatening situation,

39

whether that's a broken bone, a serious injury, or even death. Your mind receives that signal and automatically agrees with it because it's in self-preservation mode.

But if you know your body really well, you'll realise that even though you're in a lot of pain, it's not going to cross that threshold into the danger zone.

Let's say you're yomping across rough terrain with eighty or ninety pounds on your back and your body is telling you that you can't make it up the next hill, that you can't go on. If you mind doesn't take charge, then you're going to stop. But you're not injured. You haven't got a broken rib or a sprained ankle. In that situation, your body has won.

When you commit to action and expose yourself to pain on a repeated basis, you'll learn to distinguish between different pain thresholds. Going up a steep hill on Selection: that's one pain threshold. Breaking a bone is another threshold. After that it's getting shot or stabbed. But when you don't know these thresholds, you can't tell them apart. Therefore when you hit a barrier, you give up.

However, when you hit those barriers often enough, you'll learn to ignore the signals. As long as you're not physically broken, the pain you're feeling will subside. All you need to do is get used to it. You can do this by convincing your body *through your mind* that this is the specific amount of pain you're going to have to suffer before you break through it. Then that pain will become the new normal. Eventually, you'll hit a certain point, whether it's after half an hour or forty-five minutes and you'll kick back in to a new lease of life. The pain almost feels like it's disappeared. Then you'll find the strength to keep on going.

A lot of people stop before they ever reach that threshold, however. They give in to the signals their body is sending to their brain. They hold up their hands and say, 'I can't do any more. If I go on any further, I'm going to collapse or do myself a serious injury.'

But if you can turn that switch off and keep on driving through that pain, telling yourself, over and over, 'Keep going, keep going,' then you are eventually going to get through that pain barrier.

It's like rewiring a fuse board. Telling your brain to take charge of the messaging. The effect is similar to entering an ice bath. For the first sixty or ninety seconds, it's a shock to your body. Your body tells your mind, 'Get out of here!' But you stay put. Then you become accustomed to it. The body acclimatises. The same thing happens during exercise: all that's different is the length of pain you have to endure before you hit that point. It's forty-five minutes, maximum, instead of ninety seconds. But the principle is the same.

While I'm staying in that zone of pain, my body is telling me I cannot take another step. But guess what? You do take another step. Then another one. Eventually, the pain numbs, you have a renewed lease of life and your body is ready to go again.

I wasn't aware of this when I first joined the military. As a young soldier in 9 Parachute Squadron, whenever I hit the pain threshold, I stopped. I couldn't break through it because I didn't know how. And then one day we were doing an exercise in Sennybridge. Escape and evasion. The goal was to evade the Hunter Force. No time constraints. If the Hunter Force caught you, that was it.

At this point I was completely shattered. I had my Bergen on my back, probably weighing more than forty pounds. The voice flared up inside my head again.

I'm not going to make it through this one. My body's in pain, I can't move. My legs feel massacred.

Then my pal said to me, 'Ant, just keep moving.'

So I did. I pushed really, really hard. After about thirty or forty minutes, a strange thing happened. I felt ready to go again. It was like an epiphany. Something just clicked.

'Jesus,' I thought, 'how am I still going?'

After a while we reached the bank of a river. My mate shouted at me to stop so we could fill up our water bottles. I wasn't interested. I was worried that if I stopped moving for a second, that good feeling would evaporate.

That's the first time I pushed through that barrier. Broke the back of the pain threshold. It wasn't a major exercise. But it didn't matter. You don't have to climb Mount Everest or run a marathon about pain: you just have to push through *your* pain barrier. *Your* own personal threshold.

When it comes to pain, the only battle is with yourself.

Even then I didn't truly understand the pain barrier. All I had done was surprise myself by finishing the exercise strongly. It was only when I joined the Royal Marines and started doing harder yomps with more weight on my back, and later on during Selection, that I realised there are certain pain barriers, and you can actually feel them coming.

I'd get to a stage of the tab, and my body would start up with the same old routine. Firing those pain signals to my brain. 'You can't go on. You can't continue. You need to stop before something bad happens.' I knew a pain barrier was coming up, and if I just kept on going I'd eventually get a new lease of life. Whenever my body screamed at me to stop, I wouldn't give in. 'Get lost,' I'd tell it. 'I *know* I can go on.'

To do this, you have to know your body inside out. That means pushing it to its absolute limits. Learning to tell the difference between life-threatening pain and your body's early-warning system.

It's not about beating the clock or being first across the line. You could finish sixtieth in the race, or last – whatever, it doesn't matter. Everyone has a different pain threshold. Only you know your body. Only you know when you're going to get through this barrier. But if you're going to break through the barriers, you need to know your body inside out.

In my career I've had to constantly push through the pain barriers. On the hardest training exercises, I've gone through three or even more pain barriers in a single day. But I *knew* they were coming. I could anticipate them. Prepare for them. Each time, I knew that I had a maximum of an hour's work before the pain numbed again. So it became a matter of endurance.

'Get through the next sixty minutes,' I told myself. 'Survive that, and you'll be good to go.' Then I'd try to make up as much ground as possible while I still felt good.

I knew my body, I knew I could get through the pain. I had the experience of doing it before, so I knew what was physically possible. I just had to keep pushing.

The old cliché about pain being temporary – it's true. Pain is just a blip. It's something that you can choose to amplify in your mind, to the point where it crushes you. Or you can get through it.

WHEN YOUR BODY IS TELLING YOU TO GIVE UP, YOUR MIND IS POWERFUL ENOUGH TO COUNTER THOSE MESSAGES. YOUR MIND CAN TELL YOUR BODY TO KEEP GOING.

That depends to a large extent on your state of mind at the time. Are you in a good headspace? If not, then you're going to quit. To punch through that barrier you have to go in with the mindset that you're going to continue no matter what. Making sure you're in the right frame of mind is the key to embracing pain.

When your body is telling you to give up, your mind is powerful enough to counter those messages. Your mind can tell your body to keep going. But if you have a negative mindset, you'll get angry and frustrated. You'll be on the downward slope that leads, inevitably, towards accepting failure.

Before you attempt a physical challenge, ask yourself, 'How well do I know my body? How well do I know *myself*?'

The first few times I broke the barrier, I didn't even realise it had happened. I just knew that one minute I had been utterly dead on my legs and the next I felt like I could have gone on forever. It was only later, when I had time to reflect on it and break it down, that I realised what I'd done.

When you hit that barrier, don't stop. Don't give in to your body. Take control of the messaging in your mind. Tell yourself to keep going.

If you're training for a physical challenge, whether that's a triathlon or a marathon, get to know your body and what you're capable of. Learn to recognise each time you feel a pain barrier coming on, and push through it.

THE DEVIL'S THORNS

When Shaka became chief of the Zulus in 1816, they were a tiny clan, numbering maybe 2,000 people at most. Shaka had no standing army, and his territory was so small that a person could have walked from one end of it to the other in a couple of hours. Which makes it even more incredible that he transformed the Zulus into one of history's most feared armies.

When he took over, Shaka immediately drafted in the entire adult male population, roughly five hundred individuals. He also banned the new warriors from wearing sandals, because he felt that a Zulu could move faster over the ground barefoot. That didn't stop some of the older men from moaning, of course. So Shaka decided to teach them a lesson.

One day he gathered his regiments on the parade ground. Beforehand Shaka had some of the ground covered with devil's thorns – a native plant with a pair of really sharp points sticking out of the fruit. Then Shaka told his warriors to stamp on the horns with their bare feet. Anyone who hesitated or didn't look enthusiastic about the task was clubbed to death; the rest managed to stamp out the thorns and learned a valuable lesson about pain: when you're confronted by pain, you have to go through it. There's no point avoiding it, or trying to take it slowly.

By stamping out the thorns, the recruits had taken their first steps to becoming hardened Zulu warriors.

'War is the province of physical exertion and suffering. In order not to be completely overcome by them, a certain strength of body and mind is required, which, either natural or acquired, produces indifference to them.'

Carl von Clausewitz, On War, Book I, Chapter 3

DON'T REST ON YOUR LAURELS

I loved being a soldier. The commitment to discipline, knowing your craft, feeding the obsession. But I was always mindful of becoming complacent.

The moment you master something – the moment you start thinking, 'This is easy' – you have two choices. You can stay where you are and become complacent. Stop challenging yourself. Or you can ask yourself, 'What's next? What's the next challenge?'

For me, that moment arrived shortly after I'd finished my third tour.

I was in New Zealand at the time. I suddenly realised that I didn't want to stick around the unit any longer. I was done. I'd conquered that height. I wanted to move on to the next mountain. It seemed like the right time to get out.

I made my mind up there and then. 'Once I get back, I'm handing in my chit.'

We are all problem-solvers. And we're doing it constantly, hundreds of times a day, whether it's commuting to the office or taking the dog out for a walk. A lot of the time we don't even realise we're doing it. The process is so familiar to us that it becomes automatic. The only question is: What level do you want to be at? Do you want to be continually learning and growing, solving new problems? Or do you want to stay at the level of comfort?

When you've accomplished something, it's no good telling yourself, 'Well, I've done that, now I can rest on my laurels.' You have to keep pushing yourself. For me, the challenges I'm taking on now are different from the ones I faced in the army, but they're demanding in their own ways. It might involve getting up on a stage and delivering a speech to thousands of people. Or writing this book.

Unless you keep on pushing and driving, sooner or later you're going to lose your sense of purpose. There's no benchmark to measure yourself against. To keep on growing, you need to recognise who you are, what you want from life and what you need. Once you understand that, you'll begin to see what is truly going to fulfil you in all aspects of what I call the Trilogy: the emotional, the psychological and the physical. And this is a constant process. It never stops.

Challenging yourself is habit-forming. If you slacken off or start to get complacent, you'll learn to recognise the signs. I might be psychologically drained, or emotionally spent, but if I haven't tended to the physical side of things, I'll know about it.

I'll spend eight hours in the recording booth for my audiobook, for example. It's a long day. After that, all I want to do is go home, eat dinner, play with my kids and go to bed. But I can't because I haven't done anything physically challenging. I've neglected that side of the Trilogy.

I'm aware of this because I'm in tune with my body. I know when things are out of sync. Therefore, I know what to do, how to fix it.

Constantly expose yourself to hardship. Accept that there's no growth in comfort. Wherever possible, keep challenging yourself in all the ways of the Trilogy: physically, emotionally and psychologically. Instead of resting on your laurels, look to stimulate your mind and solve problems. It's what we're born to do.

CONSTANTLY EXPOSE YOURSELF TO HARDSHIP. ACCEPT THAT THERE'S NO GROWTH IN COMFORT.

If you're struggling with motivation in your career, take a step back. Ask yourself whether you're still growing and learning. If not, then you have your solution – you need to start pushing yourself.

THE SPARTAN TRAINING REGIME

The Spartans ordered their entire social system in creating a class of warriors *perpetually dedicated to the art of war*. At the bottom of the ladder were the helots – subjugated people who worked in the fields. Another group made a living as merchants and craftsmen. The Spartans fought.

Being a Spartan warrior was a lifelong commitment. Each man was expected to maintain an extremely high standard of bodily fitness and discipline throughout his life. Drunkenness was considered a sign of weakness. Spartans were forbidden from entering business. The Spartan warriors were said to be the only men who found fighting in war less knackering than training for it.

This mindset of constant exposure to hardship turned Sparta into the dominant military power among the Greeks.

Their training started very early on, actually from the moment a child was born. Shortly after birth the village elders would gather to examine the baby. If the child looked healthy, they would live. Any baby who appeared 'imperfect' or poorly in some way was left to die of exposure.

When they were seven years old, Spartan boys were organised into companies called 'herds' and subjected to a punishing regime. They trained barefoot, slept on beds made from rushes and were given miserable portions of food. To survive, they had to steal food. Those who were caught were flogged, not as a punishment, but because they had been caught in the first place.

Their adult trainers constantly pushed the Spartan youngsters, encouraging them to fight among themselves and compete at games to see how they reacted.

When they turned twenty, young Spartans became eligible for military service. This is when they applied to join one of the communal messes. Each mess had its own unique ethos and reputation, with the royal mess being at the top of the tree.

The messes were crucial to setting and maintaining standards among the Spartan warriors. Members had to provide a specified amount of food and wine each month. Unless they had a good excuse, they were expected to dine with their mess-mates every evening. They ate a plain diet including 'black broth', made from boiled pork meat and blood, flavoured with salt and vinegar. At the end of the night they made their way home without torches, so that they would learn how to rely on their natural night-vision: useful when manoeuvring in the dark on campaign.

The Spartan system of training and the special culture of the messes allowed the warriors to dedicate themselves fully to the business of fighting. They had no distractions. No one was permitted to slacken off; everyone had to maintain their individual standards and constantly push themselves and their comrades to the limits. And this system kept them sharp throughout their lives. A Spartan king called Cleomenes was once asked why they didn't wipe out the people of Argos, who were frequently waging war against them.

'We wouldn't kill them off,' Cleomenes said. 'We wanted to have some trainers for our young men.'

That determination among the Spartans to keep driving themselves on – to keep exposing themselves to hardship and danger, to avoid luxury or comfort, helped to earn them a reputation as the greatest fighting force in ancient Greece.

'Samurai's sons were let down the steep valleys of hardship, and spurred to Sisyphus-like tasks. Occasional deprivation of food or exposure to cold was considered a highly efficacious test for inuring them to endurance. Children of tender age were sent among utter strangers with some message to deliver, were made to rise before the sun, and before breakfast attend to their reading exercises, walking to their teacher with bare feet in the cold of winter; they frequently – once or twice a month, as on the festival of a god of learning – came together in small groups and passed the night without sleep, in reading aloud by turns. In the days when decapitation was public, not only were the small boys sent to witness the ghastly scene, but they were made to visit alone the place in the darkness of night and there to leave a mark of their visit on the trunkless head.'

Inazo Nitobe, The Way of the Samurai

LESSON 8

SHOW GRIT AND DETERMINATION

We called it the Bottom Field Blues.

Every Royal Marine recruit knows the feeling. The dread when you know you've got to tackle Bottom Field. You know what's coming. You're going to be carrying a heavy weight on your back, you're going to go in the tank, which is icy cold. You'll be covered from head to toe in mud.

You know you're about to be pushed way beyond your comfort zone. Beyond your limitations. Or to be more specific, the limits you have set for yourself. Therefore you become anxious. Because you don't know how your body is going to react in this situation.

Everyone suffers from the Bottom Field Blues at some point. I experienced it myself once or twice.

The reason you get the Blues is simple: you don't really know where your true limitations are until someone else pushes you to reach that point.

If you only ever rely on pushing yourself, you're never going to hit your real limitations. You'll constantly do things at your own pace, stopping and starting according to your state of mind at the time, or how tired you're feeling. You'll only manage to push yourself so far before your body or your mind tells you, 'Enough is enough. Go no further.'

But when someone else drives you on, or when a situation compels you to go on, you'll realise that you can actually function beyond your own self-imposed limits. Beyond your comfort zone. It's having an outside force telling you that you've got to be better and do better. Pushing you on until you reach the point of exhaustion. When you reach that stage, you'll grit your teeth and get through it. Then you'll get a little glimpse of how capable you are. You'll start to ask yourself, 'How tough am I? How far can I push myself?'

The more capable you become, the more you realise you can push through your boundaries. The more determined you'll be to explore those personal limits.

Soldiers are hugely comfortable with this idea. After a while, it's almost as if you no longer feel the anxiety before a tough exercise. You start telling yourself, 'It will be what it will be. I will go as far as I can go. I will push myself as hard as I possibly can before I either pass out or die.'

This push doesn't have to come from a military environment. It could equally be a situation that you've had to endure. Maybe there's a death in the family. Maybe you've lost your job, or your business has collapsed, or your house has been repossessed. Or perhaps you've been subjected to a barrage of online hate because you've dared to express an opinion.

Getting through any crisis requires immense reserves of grit and determination. It takes guts to try and find a way out. To stay strong in the face of adversity. To weather the storm, rather than lying down and giving up.

GRIT AND DETERMINATION AREN'T ABOUT SUCCEEDING IN YOUR GOALS. THEY'RE ABOUT MAKING THE JOURNEY. HAVING THE COURAGE TO SEE SOMETHING THROUGH TO THE END. IDENTIFYING THE REAL YOU.

The rawness of life identifies *true* grit and determination. But you can't explore that by yourself. It has to come from an external source.

Grit and determination aren't about succeeding in your goals. They're about making the journey. Having the courage to see something through to the end. Identifying the real you.

When you're pushed to your actual limits, you'll learn a lot about yourself. You'll know that you're going to suffer setbacks, that you're going to fail at some tasks or merely be average at others. But once you get through that process and come out on the other side, you'll realise that success and failure are both mirages. They're irrelevant. It's really about finding out who you are. That's the main reward you receive for showing grit and determination: *knowing who you are.*

In this life you have a choice between floating around, bowing down to the popular narrative and staying in your box, or gritting your teeth and getting on with it. If you have grit and determination, even though you're going to suffer, you'll be able to identify the true you. Because the more things you have to commit to – the more *uncomfortable* things you commit to – the more layers you're taking off. And therefore, the closer you will be to knowing the true version of yourself.

Confront your own Bottom Field in life. Whenever you feel the Blues before a task, tell yourself, 'This is a good thing. I'm feeling anxious because I'm about to be pushed beyond my normal limits. And I'm going to learn so much from this.'

If you find yourself hitting a wall in your fitness goals, try training with a friend or joining a group class at your local gym. When you're being pushed by someone else, whether that's a mate or a fitness instructor, you're going to be pushed much harder than if you're working alone.

THE BATTLE OF THE IMJIN RIVER

In April 1951, at the height of the Korean War, Chinese forces launched a massive assault against the 1st Battalion, Gloucestershire Regiment. The Glosters were camped out in a series of high defensive positions south of the Imjin River, roughly fifty kilometres north of the capital at Seoul, part of a larger formation guarding the west flank of the United Nations forces, strung out in a thin line twelve kilometres long. The Glosters weren't expecting serious trouble: everyone assumed the big attack would happen further east.

On the night of 22 April, it all kicked off when a blocking force engaged Chinese soldiers trying to get across the Imjin. The defenders cut down the first waves, but the enemy kept on coming and they were forced to withdraw from their position.

A short time later, A Company on Castle Hill came under attack. The fighting was brutal. Mortars splashed down on the Chinese forces crossing the river. Machine guns shredded them. Still, they kept coming, throwing more and more bodies at the defenders. The lads in A Company managed to hold their position until the following evening, when they finally withdrew and regrouped on the ridge of a nearby hill, where they were joined by some of the guys from D Company.

That night it was the turn of B and C Companies to come under huge pressure. B Company had to endure at least seven separate assaults. With the enemy closing in, the order was given for both companies to fall back, though some of the men were killed before they could link up with their mates. Others were taken prisoner. The survivors linked up with the other men on Hill 235.

Although they occupied a good position, the ground was rugged, mostly shallow soil and bedrock, and without their entrenching tools they couldn't dig trenches for cover, so they were badly exposed.

The Chinese came on again the next night. The fighting was intense. Pure chaos. Some of the Glosters were pushed off the slope before they re-attacked the Chinese and reclaimed the ground they'd lost. The next day, American jet fighters napalmed the enemy positions, but this only brought the Glosters a temporary respite from the enemy attacks.

By now it was obvious that the game was almost up. The relief column the Glosters had been told to expect wouldn't make it through in time, they were completely surrounded, they had no water or provisions, and they were down to their last rounds. Things looked totally hopeless, so they decided to stage a breakout to try and leg it through the enemy to the UN lines further south.

In the evening, the surviving defenders swept down from the hill, leaving behind the badly wounded. The men rushed across the valley floor, avoiding the surrounding slopes, which were known to be crawling with Chinese forces. Most were captured or killed before they could escape. In the end, only about one hundred and fifty managed to get away.

At the Battle of the Imjin River, the Glosters found themselves in a horrible situation. It would have been easy to lose hope and throw in the towel. But the men knew what they were about. So when the enemy came, they did what all good British soldiers do when our backs are against the wall. They showed true grit and determination.

- Personal growth is about learning. So try not to get carried away with your destination. Instead, remind yourself that every time you enter a new space, you're going to learn from the experience, no matter what.

- Practise breaking down your larger goals into smaller, more manageable phases of commitment. Approach each individual action accepting that failure is always going to be part of your journey. Be present in the moment, don't lose sight of what's in front of you and be ready to take advantage of opportunities that might come at you unexpectedly from the side.

- When the opportunity to improve is offered to you – take it. Don't hesitate.

- Seek to be consistent in your discipline. Remember that discipline is doing the things you don't want to do but know you should do – and doing them to a high standard. Understand that being consistent in your discipline is the gateway to achieving the higher realm of motivation.

- Learn to recognise the signs of complacency in yourself. When you find your standards slipping – when you become complacent – that's an early warning that you need to revert to the ways of self-discipline.

- Expose yourself to pain in your life. Put yourself through the mill. Learn more about your body and its capabilities. Pain barriers can only be broken when you tell your body, through your mind, that you can keep going, even when every part of your body is screaming at you to stop.

- Remember that there is no growth in comfort. To keep growing, you need to stimulate mind and body. In whatever you do, make sure you tick all the boxes of the Trilogy and push yourself to the limits physically, emotionally and psychologically.

- You can only identify grit and determination through someone else or an external situation pushing you to the very limits. In those moments, when you have the courage to endure what seems unendurable, you'll learn the most about yourself.

PART TWO

PLANNING AND PREPARATION

LESSON 9
YOU CANNOT BE TOO PREPARED

In the military, the mission itself is only part of a much bigger puzzle.

By far the biggest piece involves preparing for the mission. Preparation and background planning is key to mission success. On any military operation, it's vital to pull together as much intelligence as possible before you hit the ground. Otherwise you're going to run into trouble.

It's a constant process. Like discipline, you have to be *consistent* with your preparation. Consistency is all about building fundamental habits. Performing certain actions repeatedly until they become second nature to you. As every good soldier knows, being prepared today doesn't mean that you're ready for tomorrow. You have to commit to that effort continually. And that means being honest with yourself.

Preparation, at its most essential level, is about being open with your plans and with your teammates or colleagues. Identifying what you don't know and either gleaning more information or adapting your plans accordingly. Being prepared in the workplace will provide you with the mindset to deal with stress, be more engaged, and become more productive with the task at hand. It will build a resilience that will help you positively deal with pressure, setbacks, challenges and changes.

In the military, you're encouraged to embrace this attitude to its maximum.

Preparation is always key to mission success and this level of preparation might seem like overkill to anyone in the civilian world. But in the military, failing to prepare as fully as possible can cost lives.

That's why so much effort is invested in the planning phase. So when your boots hit the ground, you know you're as ready as you can be. That will give you an edge over your opponent. You'll get a psychological boost from knowing that you've left no stone unturned.

When you're preparing for a challenge in life, don't waste a moment. Spend every single second making life easier for yourself. When you take on that task, or begin that project, or face that opponent in the arena, it should almost feel like you're at home – you should be that familiar with the situation. Remember: You cannot be too prepared.

If you're preparing for a big job interview, make sure you find out as much about the role as possible beforehand. If you have a big presentation, make sure you know what you're planning to say and have answers to potential questions. Or if you're planning to go to the gym early in the morning, get your kit ready the night before to make things easier when you wake up. Preparation is the key to success. Deep down you will know if you have prepared for something. You will feel confident and ready. And that confidence will breed success.

PAY ATTENTION TO DETAIL

Attention to detail feeds into good decision-making. If one is weak, the other will be as well.

Whatever goal you're aiming for in life, the more informed you are about the challenge ahead of you, the more likely you are to complete the mission.

We embraced this attitude every day in the military. We understood that the accumulation of hundreds or even thousands of bits of information was critical to the overall success of the operation.

Planning is about asking questions. Gleaning as much information as possible. The more you know, the more you can prepare yourself – and the greater your chances of gaining a small but significant edge. This is true whether you're negotiating a business contract, buying a house or leading a team.

In the military, attention to detail is especially important because if you make a mistake or screw up in some way, there are serious and potentially life-threatening consequences. That might involve asking questions about the environment you're going into, or the favoured tactics of the enemy, right down to the tiniest detail. This is super-important because it gives you a huge boost in terms of psychologically preparing yourself for the mission. You'll know what's coming, because you'll be better prepared about the nature of the obstacle or task in front of you.

Attention is a force multiplier. The more you know, the greater the psychological advantage you're giving yourself. Because you're going to be in the right headspace. You'll be a better operator – and by extension, you're enhancing the overall performance of the team.

If I'm confident in myself – if I'm smashing through buildings and doing the business – the lads behind me are going to pick up on that. It's going to give them a buzz. Boost their own performance.

THE MORE YOU KNOW, THE GREATER THE PSYCHOLOGICAL ADVANTAGE YOU'RE GIVING YOURSELF.

On the other hand, if I'm coming off the back of the chopper in a dust-storm at night and I run off in the wrong direction, or hit the wrong compound, that's going to corrode morale. The guys will be rightly thinking, 'Jesus, talk about starting off on the wrong foot. What's Ant playing at?' Then you've got a huge task on your hands building up the confidence of your teammates from scratch. So you'd better know what you're doing.

When I disembarked from that chopper as point man, I had to make sure that my head was squared away. That I was ready for the challenge. To get into that headspace, you've got to be as fully prepared as possible. Every detail matters.

That meant preparation of self as well. Weapons, for example. I'd have to decide beforehand whether to take a smaller calibre rifle or a larger calibre piece, depending on the nature of the target.

You can hit someone with two or three rounds of smaller calibre ammo, but unless you shoot them through the head, there's a decent chance they'll bounce back up onto their feet. But when you hit a target with a higher calibre round, they're definitely going down. And staying down.

Attention to detail also means being aware of your mates or colleagues. Knowing each other's habits and preferences. If one of my pals saw my secondary weapon, for example, he'd automatically know that I had either suffered a stoppage, the dreaded dead man's click, or there had been a malfunction with my primary weapon. So we might decide to hold our position while I cleared the stoppage. Little things like this are super-important in combat.

When you have a hyper-focused group of individuals who have prepared themselves, down to the very smallest detail, the team as a whole will gain a psychological advantage.

When you're in the military, you're playing for high stakes. Every decision matters. Every piece of equipment you take.

How we're going to operate on the ground. The formation we're using. What the terrain is like. Every aspect of the mission is studied in forensic detail.

That's why attention to detail is so important. It'll help you gain that small but decisive edge. That extra one or even half a per cent. Being detail-orientated, you can achieve great things. You'll be able to reach your goals in less time and with less effort. You will avoid mistakes. And you'll increase your efficiency. It will also positively affect your relationships with those around you. You'll be able to communicate clearly and build stronger connections in the process. It's also going to give you and your teammates a confidence boost as a result.

ELIMINATE DISTRACTIONS

A huge part of mentally preparing yourself for a goal or challenge involves keeping your head in the game *at all times*.

I used to tell myself, 'I'm the best soldier in the world. No one out there can out-soldier me.'

But telling yourself that you're the best is pointless unless you back it up with unrelenting dedication to the task.

Whatever you set your mind to – whether it's capturing a target, sealing a business deal, or going for a job interview – you have to be fully focused on that objective, to the point where there are zero psychological or emotional distractions. What I mean by that is, you can't have something else taking up room in your head, because that will only hinder your performance. Anything external to your goal has got to go.

I prepared myself for the battlefield by making sure that I never let a seed of doubt enter my head. I turned my mind into a fortress. Any distractions that came knocking on the door, I got rid of them. Banished them from my head. From the moment I began my tour, I took my family hat off and put my military hat on.

Other guys handled the pressures of combat tours differently. They liked to stay in touch with their loved ones, but I didn't see that as being helpful. For me, family life was a distraction from my job. It stopped me from keeping my head in the game. So I went the other way. I didn't get my family to write to me. I didn't want to know if the kids were misbehaving or if the dishwasher had packed up. I gave my wife a number to reach me in case of an emergency, but otherwise I didn't want to know.

My wife was incredibly good at helping me to stay focused. If I did call her up, she'd tell me that the kids were great, everything was fine – even though that probably wasn't the case. But she knew I couldn't afford to carry that distraction into a mission. She allowed me to be fully focused at all times. I was able to leave my civilian self behind. Detach myself from civilisation, in a way, to the point where it felt like I was living in a completely different world.

Eliminating distractions goes hand in hand with compartmentalisation. The ability to purge stuff from your mind is absolutely key in the military. You have to be able to put all the other stuff in a box and focus on the mission.

I might be pissed off with one of my pals, for example. Perhaps they'd messed up on a previous mission. I'd be rightly furious with them, and at the appropriate moment I'd let them know that they had messed up. But as soon as we stepped on to the battlefield, we were brother warriors once more. I'd take it as a personal insult if someone was firing at that guy. Then we'd get back to base, have the debrief and that mindset would go. Like flicking a switch. When the job was done, I probably wouldn't talk to that person for another week.

As soon as you enter the arena, or go into the big meeting, make sure your head is wholly focused on the job. Leave everything else behind.

LESSON 12

DON'T MAKE ASSUMPTIONS

Assumption is the enemy of good preparation. When we looked at a target prior to the operation, we followed a simple rule. Only act on things we have *seen*.

If we haven't seen it, if there's a grey area where information isn't available for whatever reason, or it's scanty, then we can't be absolutely sure about it. Until we can confirm something with our eyes and ears, we'll approach with caution. In which case, we'll proceed carefully.

If it later turns out to be a threat, based on what we've seen and heard, we can modify the plan accordingly. But we never make assumptions.

This is why having boots on the ground is still massively important. You can have all the drones and intelligence platforms in the world, but you cannot replicate the intelligence value of a human operator looking at things in real-time. A picture is open to interpretation. It can be unreliable or misleading. Technology is unreliable. Mistakes can be made. And that can potentially compromise a mission – sometimes fatally.

In high-risk situations, you can only truly trust your eyes and ears.

That mindset of not relying on assumptions was equally important when it came to gathering information. What we saw on the ground was taken as gospel and fed into a network that cost billions of dollars and took years to build. People have this image of soldiers being all about action. Crack open the armoury, grab a weapon and go. But gathering intel was actually a core part of our duties.

But any system is only as good as the information being plugged into it. So it became super-important for us to be sure about our intel.

Our modus operandi was: *Don't assume things.* If you're not one hundred per cent sure about something, then don't say it. Better to be silent than to assume. Because if you're feeding Chinese whispers into a highly complex network, eventually you're going to send someone into a trap.

Whatever you set out to do in life, arm yourself with credible information. When that isn't available, proceed cautiously. Don't settle for assumptions. Whenever you substitute knowledge for assumptions, you're going into a situation without being fully aware of what is in front of you.

'Be like a promontory against which the waves are always breaking. It stands fast, and stills the waters that rage around it.'

Marcus Aurelius, Meditations, Book 4.49

MAKE SURE YOUR HOUSE IS IN ORDER

In the military I was fixated on making sure my kit was ready at all times. It became an obsession.

There's a good reason for this. We were doing a lot of time-sensitive missions, which meant we didn't always have time to thoroughly check our kit before moving on to the next target. So whenever we came back from a mission, the very first thing I did was make sure I was on top of my game. Get my house in order. And it started with cleaning my weapons.

I had a good cleaning routine going. I'd decompress the springs in my magazines for an hour or two. I felt this was important because for the kind of ops we were doing, we'd rarely get through more than a few rounds. We were unlikely to chew through four or six mags on a single mission. But if you don't empty the rounds from a clip – if the spring stays compressed for a long time – that can affect the motion of the bullets being pushed up into the chamber. Weapon performance becomes degraded. Worst case scenario, you might suffer a stoppage. Dead man's click. In the heat of a firefight, that can be fatal.

So after each job I'd methodically take the rounds out of the magazines on my primary weapon, relieving the pressure on the springs. I'd oil the clips, clean the weapon thoroughly, reload the mags into the feed. Then I'd head down to the range and loose off a few rounds. In my head, I was breaking the weapon in. I'd make sure that all the parts were in good working order, that the weapon felt right in my grip.

I'd do the same thing with my pistol, too. I kept right on top of it, made sure that it was clean as a whistle.

Between each mission I used to keep all my operational kit locked away in a cage outside my room: primary weapon, anything I might need for the job. I'd have spare batteries for every bit of gear. I'd have a compass in there as well. I was obsessed with maintaining everything in that cage.

But here's the thing. You have to allow yourself to be obsessed. Create the mindset necessary for that obsession. Because I'd cleared my mind of distractions, I had created the headspace to become fixated on my equipment. I didn't have to fret about the kids, or problems with the house. My mind was free to concentrate on my immediate situation. My head was in the game, instead of worrying about something happening thousands of miles away.

Squaring away my kit became a vital mental exercise. When all my equipment was good to go, that meant my head was squared away too. I felt ready for whatever the next mission might throw at me.

My country had invested a serious amount of money in

training us; in return, they expected us to risk our lives in some of the most dangerous places on the planet. And some of us would have to make the ultimate sacrifice. I took this responsibility very seriously. I knew that not all of the guys on my team would make it back home.

I was ready for that. I accepted it. I had already mentally prepared myself for whatever I was going to see. It might sound strange, but when I knew in my own head that I'd sorted my kit, that I'd studied the target, knew them inside out, better than they knew themselves – all of that allowed me to put the fear of dying to one side. Making sure my house was in order was key to approaching a mission in the right mindset.

Preparation begins with the self. You'll struggle to accomplish anything if your house isn't in order. Sort out the things within your control and you'll be well on the way to sorting out your headspace.

KEEP IT SIMPLE

Whatever the task, make sure you build from the bottom up. Don't begin with complexity. If you look too far ahead, if you start from the end-point to arrive at your solution, you're going to make the mistake of overplanning.

I like to compare it to driving a car. You don't begin by thinking, 'How do I get this thing up to a hundred miles per hour?' You start by asking, 'How do I get this car to *one* mile an hour? How do I get it up and running in the first place?' Once you're on the move, you can figure it out. Solve each further problem as you go along.

When we did a mission, we never looked at the orders process in its totality. If you did that, you'd think, 'Bloody hell, there are a lot of moving parts there, there's a lot to remember.'

We approached the mission from the other direction. We'd simplify it by focusing on the first action. We'd say to ourselves, 'Right, let's tick that first box.' That first step or commitment. Don't focus too far ahead.

Whatever happens after that first step, we're going to trust in our drills and skills to find a way through. We might throw another element into the mix. Charlie Team might be told, 'You're going in first. We'll start by clearing building Alpha One.' It would be nice to tackle those buildings in chronological order, moving on to Alpha Two and then Alpha Three, the situation might mean that we have to jump ahead and go straight to Alpha Five instead. There's no point trying to come up with a comprehensive solution before we hit the ground.

Always approach a problem by asking yourself, 'How can I get this moving? Where does this puzzle start?' Once you know that, you can start actioning it. And once you've actioned something, the ball is rolling. You're on the way. That first commitment will automatically lead on to the next commitment, and so on.

As long as you've got the overall picture of where you need to be in your head, you'll figure out the details as you go.

A lot of people want the full solution laid out in front of them before they're prepared to commit to anything. They don't trust themselves to solve problems along the way. But this approach is deeply flawed because the moment you attack a plan, the moment the process in your head makes contact with hard reality, it's going to change. There are going to be failures along the way. At which point you'll need to improvise or rethink your approach.

Keep it simple. *Beginning, middle, end.*

ALWAYS APPROACH A PROBLEM BY ASKING YOURSELF, 'HOW CAN I GET THIS MOVING? WHERE DOES THIS PUZZLE START?'

Focus on the beginning first. Trust yourself to action the next steps once you reach them. Don't try to plot out every step of commitment or action between the beginning and the middle, or the middle and end.

Commit solely to the starting point.

The end-goal is mission success, of course. But even if you don't hit that goal, at the very least you've committed to the actions necessary to reach that end point. And you'll be fascinated by what you'll learn from yourself during the journey. The rewards and goals from that initial commitment are mind-blowing.

Overplanning can stop you from taking that first step. What people often do is become fixated on solving the problem in a very specific way. The moment it doesn't go according to plan as they have visualised it or mapped it out, they ditch the project. They tell themselves, 'This can't be done.' They push the project to one side because it didn't go completely according to plan. They've failed to remember the most important lesson of problem-solving: *there are many different paths you can take to reach the solution.* There's no one set way to complete the puzzle or succeed in the mission.

When you're faced with a complex plan, take a step back. Revert to simplicity. Remind yourself that you only need to understand how you're going to get something started. Rather than wasting precious time and resources planning out the whole project step-by-step, focus on that initial action.

After that, you'll figure it out for yourself.

If you've got a good team behind you, with the right attitude and approach to life, you're going to get the job done.

Managing a big project at work can make you feel anxious. That's perfectly normal. Here's how to reduce that anxiety: instead of trying to map the whole thing out in your head, focus only on the first steps involved in that project. Trust in your ability to solve problems as you go along.

LESSON 15

DELEGATE TASKS

Within the SF community, you learn to appreciate the support units around you.

In the conventional military forces, everything is done in-house, more or less. But at the elite level, you're part of a multi-agency approach. On the ground, there are people responsible for carrying out specific tasks in support of the overall mission. Each support team is a vital cog in the overall machine.

But in order to let them do their jobs, you have to get out of the way. They're the specialists in their particular field, so let them get on with it. And trust that they're on top of their own game. As soldiers, we were fortunate enough to be surrounded by elite-performance teams. That allowed us the mental head-space to concentrate on our tasks, knowing that they had our backs.

It's no good trying to micro-manage a military operation. You have to delegate zones of responsibility. Trust in the abilities of your muckers to get you out of a fix if the worst happens.

Of course, it's important to know each other's tasks so you

can coordinate effectively on the ground. If you're in charge of the assets in the sky, for example, you need to know their roles inside-out. Then you can make a decision on how you should utilise those assets prior to the assault – or whether you need them at all.

But you can only reach that decision through a combination of experience and understanding the capabilities of the other assets and trusting in them to deliver.

Trust isn't optional in this situation. You *have* to trust them. If they don't do the job, there's nothing you can do about it.

The same thing is true for the individual teams on the ground. Each person has a specific field of responsibility. You can't tell them what to do every step of the way. You've just got to trust in your teammates' skills and training to get the team through the mission.

Don't micro-manage. Don't interfere. Instead, make the effort to know each other's tasks. Learn to hand over responsibility to others, and the team will benefit.

There are times, of course, when you have no option but to do the job yourself.

This actually happened to us on a mission once. We were going out on ops with another team who weren't as good as us. These guys weren't up to scratch. They were so useless, we'd get them to clear rooms and they'd stumble back out having been shot in the arse or the backplate.

In the end, this became too hazardous. It made more sense to gather the TLs (Team Leaders) together and clear the building ourselves. We'd tell the lads on the other team, 'You lot can secure the perimeter.' Leave them outside and go and get the job done between us. It was a case of going, 'Sod the rules. We've got to prioritise our mission and our lives.'

When it comes to leading, trust your judgement. Understand your teammates' individual capabilities and limitations. When you truly know your team, what makes them tick and their individual personalities, you'll learn to understand when to assert control – and when to take a step back and delegate responsibility. Avoid falling into the trap of micromanagement. Trust them to do their jobs. And back yourself to do yours.

LESSON 16

USE YOUR TIME EFFICIENTLY

The art of good planning is about maximising the limited time available to you and your team to acquire as much information as possible on your goal.

On a time-sensitive mission there might only be a very short window in which to act. We had to be ready to jump into action at a moment's notice. In those situations we didn't have the luxury of planning a mission for days beforehand. We had to act immediately. So it became a case of relying on our well-honed drills and skills, the homework we'd previously done on the target, and using what little time we had left to gather critical information related to the mission and sketch out a quick plan. There was no time to thrash out something very complicated or detailed. We'd just cover the basics, the bare bones.

WHEN YOU SET
YOURSELF TO A
TASK, MAXIMISE
YOUR TIME. EVEN
IF THERE'S ONLY
A TINY WINDOW,
USE THAT
OPPORTUNITY TO
YOUR ADVANTAGE.
FIND OUT AS MUCH
AS YOU CAN ABOUT
THE OBJECTIVE.
MAKE EVERY
SECOND COUNT.

This is where preparation becomes really important. We didn't need to waste valuable time before the op preparing our kit or orientating ourselves with the general environment. Because we'd already done our homework.

When you set yourself to a task, maximise your time. Even if there's only a tiny window, use that opportunity to your advantage. Find out as much as you can about the objective. Make every second count.

If you're working to a tight deadline, don't complicate things by taking on too much. Strip everything back and focus on the basics. Use your time positively, rather than allowing the panic or stress to win.

'Only remember the distinction between what is your own and what is not your own, and you will never claim what belongs to others. Judicial bench or dungeon, each is but a place, one high, the other low; but your will is equal to either condition, and if you have a mind to keep it so, it may be so kept.'

Epictetus, Discourses, Book II, 6.24–25

- Prepare yourself as much as possible for the task ahead. When you set out to complete the project or event, the situation should be so familiar it should almost feel like being at home: that's the level of preparation you should look to achieve.

- Whatever you do, remember that details matter. When you pay attention to the small things, each tiny percentage point will give you an edge – and therefore improve your chances of completing the overall bigger mission or goal.

- Banish distractions from your mind. A distracted mind will only hinder your ability to get the job done and perform to a high standard. Make sure you're fully focused on the meeting or op in front of you.

- Never rely on assumptions. When you don't know some-thing, when you don't have credible information, don't assume. Either find out more about what's in front of you or adjust your plans accordingly.

- Keep your house in order. Exert control over the things within your reach. Preparation always begins with yourself.

- Build your objectives or aims from the bottom up. Don't over-complicate things by trying to map out the entire task inside your head before you begin. Instead, start with the first step. The initial action. Trust in yourself to figure it out from there. Always look to keep things simple.

- Don't try to micro-manage the people on your team. Trust in their skills and training to see the mission through. Make sure everyone understands each other's roles and responsi-bilities. Remind yourself that delegating tasks is vital to the greater success and growth of the whole team.

- Most of all, be efficient with your time-management. Use whatever limited time you have to maximise your advantage. Even a small window can mean the difference between victory and success if you make the effort to use it.

PART THREE

THE COMBAT ZONE

FOCUS, NOT FRUSTRATION

At the elite level, military operations call for a lot of patience
– and focus.

A soldier might have to wait hours or days for a target.
During the Malaya Emergency in the 1950s, fought between
British Empire and Commonwealth forces and the Communist
insurgents of the Malayan National Liberation Army (MNLA),
the SAS (reconstituted after the end of the Second World
War) would spend hours or even days in dense jungle observing dead-letter drop locations used by the enemy. They'd sit
and wait, biding their time until a Communist Terrorist (CT)
showed up to pick up or deposit a message.

During those periods, it's easy for a soldier to get bored or
frustrated. That's where discipline comes in.

Without discipline, focus can easily bleed into frustration.
Once you become frustrated, you create a disconnect.
Whenever there's a disconnect, there's a break in the circuitry
that someone else can exploit. A chink in the armour. A
vulnerability, waiting to be attacked.

I always used to tell the guys on my team, 'Don't ever let the enemy see you getting frustrated.'

There's a massive psychological advantage in seeing focus give way to frustration. As soon as you see that disconnect in your opponent, you know you've got him right where you want him.

Whenever I'd see that break, I'd think to myself, 'Okay, I'm coming for you now.' Once my opponent had revealed a weakness, I knew I could get in there and use that weak link to defeat him. It was a small but important victory in my head.

This is equally true in elite-level sport. When players get frustrated, they tend to let it show – and it gives the other side a boost.

Except in battle, that moment of weakness might cost you your life.

I saw this happen many times myself. Sometimes we'd find ourselves up against a group of hardened enemy combatants. In those cases, we knew we had to be patient. That was the key to success.

Eventually, they'd get frustrated. We'd see the tell-tale signs. It might be something as simple as the way they were moving. But we *knew*. As soon as I spotted that frustration breaking through, I felt that I'd gained a vital psychological edge over them. I'd be thinking, 'Now I've got you.'

The flip side of that is that staying focused will degrade your opponent's morale. It takes a lot of grit, courage and mental resilience not to give in to frustration, to stay in that zone of focus, especially when you're in a high-stress environment, whether that's the battlefield, or a sports arena.

Whenever we found ourselves up against an ultra-focused

enemy, I knew straight away that we'd have a serious fight on our hands. Because you're dealing with someone without a weak point. Someone in control of their emotions. Focused individuals are formidable adversaries. Someone who's laser-focused can't be goaded into making mistakes.

When that F kicks in, make sure it's Focus, not Frustration.

If you're feeling tense, or fatigued, or you're anxious, don't let anyone see that weakness because it'll leave you vulnerable. In a combat situation, if anyone is smart enough to spot that weakness, they'll take full advantage of it. The same goes for you in the workplace. People will always find a way to work through that gap. So make sure it's not there. Or keep it well hidden.

HANNIBAL AND QUINTUS FABIUS

In 217 BC, Hannibal, the brilliant Carthaginian general, crossed the Alps with a large army of mercenaries drawn from North Africa, Gaul and Spain. At Lake Trasimene, he crushed a Roman army, sending shockwaves through Rome itself.

In a state of panic, the Romans decided to appoint Quintus Fabius as dictator, with Marcus Minucius Rufus chosen as his Master of Horse.

Fabius's chances of success looked slim. Hannibal had already smashed the Romans in two major scraps. His men were seriously hard veteran warriors, confident in their own ability. Whereas the Romans were at rock bottom. Their earlier defeats had put them on the back foot. Morale was low.

Fabius was aware of this. He was the kind of bloke who dealt in realities, seeing things as they really were, not as he wanted to see them. He knew that his army would get hammered if he sought to confront Hannibal head-on. He also knew that another catastrophic defeat could have fatal implications for the defence of Italy and Rome itself.

So Fabius chose to wage a different type of war. He fought defensively, playing to his advantages in terms of manpower and logistics, denying Hannibal the opportunity to fight the large-scale battle that he craved. In this way, Fabius gave the Romans precious time to rebuild and regain their strength.

Hannibal repeatedly tried to provoke Fabius into a big fight. Each time, Fabius refused. His army shadowed the Carthaginians but at a certain distance so his men wouldn't be in danger. Rather than fighting battles they limited themselves to low-level attacks on enemy foraging parties.

This was a clever approach: Fabius was using time to grind down his enemy. He knew that time was Rome's friend. They were fighting on home soil, they had plenty of supplies, therefore they could afford to wait until the situation improved. Whereas the Carthaginians were in hostile territory, with few allies. They couldn't stick around in Italy forever. Before long Hannibal's men would be itching to go home.

Hannibal then made his first mistake. He became frustrated. He started torching the countryside, burning everything in sight in a desperate attempt to force Fabius into action. But Fabius stayed focused. He stuck to his plan because he could see it was working.

That doesn't mean it was an easy decision. All the time, Fabius had to deal with his men becoming frustrated at the lack of action. People started calling him 'The Delayer' because of what they felt was an overly defensive approach. Others accused him of cowardice. To his credit, Fabius ignored his critics. All of his energies were concentrated on preventing Hannibal from gaining the victory he desperately wanted – and needed.

Minucius happened to be one of Fabius's biggest critics. Eventually the Senate voted to award him the same powers as Fabius, effectively making him co-dictator. They agreed to split the army equally between them. With his own independent command, Minucius wasted no time in going on the front foot against Hannibal.

At the Battle of Geronium he blundered into a trap. The night before the fight, Hannibal stealthily moved some of his light infantrymen and cavalry towards the base of a hill, where they would be hidden from view amid the broken ground. At daybreak, he lured Minucius into an attack by occupying the hillock in strength.

Hannibal had studied his enemy closely. He understood how Minucius thought. He knew that Minucius was, emotionally, at the opposite end of the spectrum from Fabius. He was rash and impulsive, he didn't think things through. Hannibal was gambling on the fact that Minucius wouldn't be able to resist attacking the hilltop. He was right.

As soon as Hannibal saw that Minucius had committed his men to the attack, the Carthaginian general gave the signal. The ambushers who had been hidden in the broken ground charged out of their cover and tore into the Romans from every direction. It would have been a massacre, but the Romans were saved by Fabius's quick thinking. When he saw that Minucius was in serious trouble, Fabius gathered his men and rushed over to help him. Hannibal caught sight of the fresh troops bearing down on his position and decided to break off.

In the end, Fabius had been proved right. By sticking to a cautious strategy, using guerrilla warfare tactics, and playing to his strengths, he saved Rome from annihilation.

ELIMINATE SELF-DOUBT

Self-doubt is the enemy of the elite soldier. You can't have a shred of self-doubt going into battle.

In the military, whatever unit you're in, you are constantly being told that you're the best. There's a very good reason for this. Self-doubt is like gangrene. It's highly infectious. Unless you cut it off completely, it's going to keep on growing and consume you.

The army knows this. That's why they put so much effort into stamping it out. They don't want a seed of self-doubt in your head.

In the workplace, self-doubt might stop you from getting a promotion or sealing a big contract. An elite athlete carrying self-doubt in their heads might miss a penalty or lose a big race. But in the military, allowing self-doubt to creep in can get you killed.

I've personally seen what happens when soldiers open the door to self-doubt. Some years ago I was doing a training course in the UK prior to my next deployment, when I got a phone call from a good pal of mine. There was a distinctive edge to his voice. He was calling to say that someone I knew had been KIA.

Killed in Action.

KIAs happen, no matter how much we prepare, no matter how hard we train. I've known some very good soldiers who had elements of self-doubt about them. Guys who don't believe in themselves as much as some of the other lads. This guy had the same attitude. He felt he wasn't as good as his muckers. Probably he wasn't confident about going into certain situations. Before a mission he'd sometimes say, 'I'm not feeling this one, Ant. This doesn't feel right.' Or he'd have a sense that something bad was going to happen.

In his mind he was opening the door to self-doubt.

Consequently the self-doubt he carried around in his head became a kind of self-fulfilling prophecy. Almost as if he was marking his own card.

Self-doubt created a chink in his armour. A vulnerability. For a soldier, that vulnerability can be fatal.

YOUR ATTITUDE – YOUR MINDSET – IS CRITICAL TO DETERMINING WHETHER YOU'LL SUCCEED OR FAIL AT A GIVEN TASK.

I genuinely believe that what kept me alive was keeping self-doubt at bay. Not for one second did I ever believe that I would get shot or injured. Every time we went out on a job, I always fully believed that I would be getting back on that chopper again and returning to camp. Even when things went wrong, when we found ourselves in drastic situations, I made sure that lid of self-doubt stayed firmly closed. Because once you let it in, it can snowball very quickly.

Your attitude – your mindset – is critical to determining whether you'll succeed or fail at a given task. If you're obsessed with your craft, if you're truly passionate about achieving your goals, or becoming the best at your chosen profession, then you won't let self-doubt in because you'll be too fixated on learning from your mistakes and using those lessons to grow. Making mistakes won't affect you. But when you approach a task *expecting* to mess it up, then you've already welcomed self-doubt into your head. You've created the room for it to flourish. And it'll be that much more difficult for you to cut it off and focus on your objective.

BE LIKE THE SPARTANS

The Spartans took their craft seriously. From an early age they were trained to be bold, aggressive, cunning in battle.

When they were drawn up for battle, they didn't behave like other forces. They didn't work themselves up into a frenzy, or hurl insults at their opponents like the Celts, or beat their swords against their shields to intimidate their opponents. Instead, the Spartans advanced steadily, coolly, keeping their formation intact and moving shoulder-to-shoulder, marching to the sound of the musicians playing their reed instruments.

This was a brilliant psychological ploy. The Spartans were communicating to their enemies that they had total confidence in their skills. To advance slowly into battle, staying in complete control of yourself, is impossible unless you've banished all traces of self-doubt.

There's a thin line between confidence and delusion, however. Delusion is *unearned* confidence. It's a form of self-deception. If the Spartans hadn't properly applied themselves to the study and practice of war, and then they had drawn up for battle acting as if they had already won, they would have been deluded. To gain confidence, you have to first be prepared to graft.

Eliminate self-doubt from your mind like the Spartan warriors. Don't give self-doubt room to breathe. Focus on doing the work, be obsessed with your craft and accept that you are going to make mistakes along the way. Approach each task calmly and with a positive mindset. When you do that, good things will start to happen.

'Who is it, after all, that I fear? The master of what? Of things in my own power? Of these no one is the master. Of things not in my power? And what are these to me?'

Epictetus, Discourses, Book I, 29.8

LESSON 19

MAKE A DECISION

In today's world, it's easy to avoid making decisions. We live in a society that encourages weakness. Society tells us to look for excuses, that we should blame outside factors for the situation we find ourselves in, when in fact we should really be looking in the mirror.

Blaming outside forces for your shortcomings is a form of mental surrender. It means you're not being honest or truthful with yourself. You're surrendering *control of your mind.*

The more difficult thing to do is to take charge of your mind. Exert self-control and self-discipline.

The same is true for decision-making. A lot of people put off making decisions in their lives, because almost everything is done for them nowadays. So when they find themselves in a position where they absolutely *have* to make a call, they freeze. They can't face the situation. They're afraid of what might happen if they get it wrong. They're in unfamiliar territory. So they don't make any decision at all, or they delay it.

Or they wait for someone else to make a decision for them, which is just as bad.

They surrender control.

To take charge of your decision-making, you have to first understand the difference between *mindset triggered by emotion,* and *mindset triggered by reason.*

WHEN YOU LEARN TO NURTURE A MINDSET BASED ON REASON RATHER THAN EMOTION, YOU'LL START TO TAKE CONTROL OF THE DECISION-MAKING PROCESS.

Mindset is most often triggered by emotion. You feel an emotion – fear, for example, or distress, or joy – and you make a decision based on that. Or it can happen the other way round. You'll see or hear something, and that will trigger an emotional response, which feeds back to a decision.

Either way, you're not in full control of the process. You're allowing emotions to rule the roost.

Mindset triggered by reason is much harder to achieve, but much more rewarding.

When you learn to nurture a mindset based on reason rather than emotion, you'll start to take control of the decision-making process. You're no longer surrendering to external factors, or to a particular emotional reaction.

In the military, decision-making is massive.

Military ops are the ultimate form of problem-solving exercise. Except it's not about getting a high score at the end of it or winning a prize. The stakes are much higher. You're either going to live, or you're going to die.

Whether you're a young operator or an experienced soldier, you're going to find yourself in situations where you need to make a call, quickly, sometimes in a split-second – and you need to be able to live with that decision for the rest of your life. The wrong call might get you or your mates killed. Or result in a mission failure.

That's where adaptability comes in. Elite soldiers need to be flexible enough to make a decision on the spot, even when we didn't have all the information to hand. Mission planning can only take you so far. What you have at the planning stage is the mission in skeleton form. The role of any elite team is to put meat on the bones of the job, in real-time.

If you're going to thrive in that situation, you can't be fazed by the unknown. You have to embrace it, see it as a challenge. A test of your versatility, your emotional intelligence and psychological resilience. Can you figure this thing out for yourself and deal with it? Because that's what happens on a mission. You're thrown in at the deep end, into a compound or a village. Suddenly you've got a fraction of a second to figure it out. It's sink or swim.

Ultimately, however, *any* decision is better than none.

In my heart of hearts, I always felt that if the decision I'd taken was the right one to make *at that specific moment in time*, given what I knew, then I could live with it – even if it later turned out to be the wrong one. The way I looked at it was this: at least I'd made a decision. If it was the right one, great. If I got it wrong, then I could rectify it later on. Make a new – and better – decision. But either way, at least I've done *something*. I've been proactive. I haven't been standing around with a thumb up my arse, surrendering control.

Leadership in the workplace is ultimately about making decisions. When you're confronted with a difficult situation, don't hesitate. Make a decision, based on the information in front of you. If you get it wrong, you get it wrong. But at least you did something. And that's always better than doing nothing.

PREFECT POSTUMUS AND THE CONSEQUENCES OF INDECISION

When rebellion erupted in Roman Britain in AD 60, Governor Paulinus rushed to assemble the legions to meet the enemy. His forces were scattered across the province, so Paulinus sent word to the Second Legion, based in Exeter, to join him as soon as possible.

The commanding officer of this legion happened to be away at the time, so responsibility fell onto the shoulders of Poenius Postumus, the camp prefect. (Camp prefects were very experienced soldiers, in charge of all the admin and logistics.)

This was a critical moment in the uprising. Paulinus had a full-blown revolt on his hands. Part of one of the four legions under his command had been cut to pieces in a clash with the enemy. He needed every available soldier in the province if he was to stand any chance of defeating the rebels.

But Postumus failed to rise to the occasion. Instead of leaving the garrison to link up with Paulinus's army, he hesitated. He did nothing. Perhaps he feared an uprising from the nearby tribes if he moved his men away from the fort. Maybe he had faulty intelligence which suggested the rest of the province had already been lost. Maybe he was afraid of getting ambushed en-route. We'll never know.

What's clear is that Postumus made the wrong choice.

In the end, the Romans won the day even without the help of their friends in the Second Legion. Postumus later committed suicide. Instead of giving his men the chance to share in the glory of victory, his inaction cost him his reputation – and his life.

Even if he thought that the rest of the army had been defeated, Postumus had options on the table. He could have sent his men out to assert control over the surrounding area. Bang heads, arrest any troublemakers and gather intel on the situation elsewhere. Make sure his own little corner of the province was under control. Improve the fort's defences. Send for help across the Channel to Gaul. Anything would have been better than staying put and doing nothing.

Avoid making the same mistake as Postumus in your life. Inaction is no substitute for a decision. Commit to doing something proactive, rather than nothing. No one ever achieved anything in life by standing still.

LESSON 20

MAKE YOUR EMOTIONS WORK FOR YOU

Most people are familiar with the physical and mental requirements of being a good soldier. But there's another component which is just as important, even though it's rarely discussed: emotional intelligence.

Emotional intelligence is crucial in forging today's warfighters.

But it's often misunderstood. We tend to focus on suppressing emotions. It's common to hear people say things like, 'Don't get emotional,' or, 'Don't let your emotions run away from you.' This is rooted in a failure to understand a basic truth of emotions: you have no control over how and when they present themselves.

If someone insults you in the street, that might trigger an emotion, and you can't help that. That emotion is going to present itself regardless. You might tell yourself to brush it off, to ignore it – not to react to it – but that doesn't change the core fact of the emotion itself. It will still be there, burning in your chest. And if you don't understand that process, what you're feeling and why, that emotion is going to work against you.

Emotional fitness means getting to grips with your emotions. When you do this, you'll learn to take charge of your emotions – and get them to work for you.

When people fail to do this, they often fall into the trap of their minds playing tricks on them, because they can't tell the difference between emotions triggered by a situation, and emotions triggered by the mind. Their bodies and minds aren't in harmony.

Before we can unpick this, we need to recognise that thought processes are different to feelings. A feeling is an immediate response to something. Imagine you're in a shopping centre with your kid. All of a sudden you turn around, you can't see your child anywhere, and the fear suddenly hits you. *My child is missing.* The air traps in your throat. You feel like you can't breathe.

That feeling has been triggered because you genuinely believe your son or daughter has vanished – and you have absolutely zero control over that emotion. It can't be deleted or silenced.

Unfortunately, we have a horrible tendency of working that same process in reverse. Take fear. If you're claustrophobic, the thought of going into an underground cave will probably be enough to trigger a reaction. You're not actually in a confined space at that moment in time. But merely visualising yourself in that cave will stimulate an emotional response. The mind is playing tricks on you. It's triggering an emotion for a situation that isn't real.

Emotions triggered when we are confronted with external events are natural. *Artificial* emotions occur when we visualise or perceive a situation that only exists internally, in our heads.

Typically, people aren't even aware that their minds are working against them. They're so consumed by the emotion that's been triggered that they don't realise their brains are actively engaged in manufacturing these emotional and physical responses.

This tends to happen when people overthink. High-achieving individuals or people in high-performance teams often fall into this trap because they're more likely to over-analyse something. This is what I call adaptability in reverse. You're making yourself less adaptable, limiting what you might achieve, merely by overthinking.

This is how our bodies work. The emotion always comes first. Feeling precedes the thought process. Emotion there-fore plays a key role in how we behave. How we react when we're faced with certain situations. And although we can't control when or how our emotions present themselves, we *can* influence our responses to them. The way we choose to interpret them.

Think of your emotions as a physical thing, like weapons in an armoury. Nine times out of ten, when an emotion presents itself, we don't take the time to look at it in detail. We panic and put it back in the armoury because we don't want to open it up and confront it.

In the military, we had to be able to take charge of our emotions, not let ourselves be directed by them. I'd never allow myself to be directed by anger when planning or execut-ing an op. Anger is useless in that type of situation. It won't help you achieve mission success. If you're not in complete control of your emotions, you're going to spiral very rapidly into a negative mindset.

Strive for emotional intelligence in your interactions with your friends and colleagues. Every time you're faced with an emotion, take the time to analyse it. Recognise it for what it is, where it's come from, why you're feeling that way, and you'll be in a position to make a conscious decision on how to make that emotion work for you. Don't let the emotion take control and lead you on blindly.

TAKE CONTROL OF YOUR ACTIONS

Commitment to action is only the first part of the battle to better yourself. In order to gain self-belief, you need to learn from the action. And to learn from the action, you need to be in complete control of it.

What I mean by that is, a positive commitment to action has to be made during the *entire* action. Otherwise, you're surrendering control at least partly to an outside force. When you commit to only part of an action, you aren't giving yourself the opportunity to learn from it and gain that glimmer of self-belief.

Take skydiving, for example. Someone once said to me, 'I've conquered my fear of heights, Ant.'

'What do you mean you've conquered your fear?' I asked.

This person explained that he had been petrified of heights, but he had recently completed a skydive, and now he was no longer afraid.

'What did you do, exactly?' I asked.

'Well, I jumped out of the plane,' he replied.

'Were you in control of that action?'

'No,' he said. 'It was a tandem skydive.'

Now, in a tandem skydive, you're strapped to an instructor. They're the ones in real control of the action. They're in charge of the jump out of the aircraft; they control the descent and landing. All the other person did was keep their eyes clamped shut the whole time.

WHEN YOU COMMIT TO ONLY PART OF AN ACTION, YOU AREN'T GIVING YOURSELF THE OPPORTUNITY TO LEARN FROM IT AND GAIN THAT GLIMMER OF SELF-BELIEF.

'Then you haven't conquered anything,' I said. 'You've probably got used to heights, but you haven't conquered them. They're two different things. It's not like you threw yourself out the plane and had control of your opening and steering and landing.'

Then I asked him whether he would go up again and jump by himself, without an instructor. This guy looked at me wide-eyed. 'Of course I wouldn't,' he replied. 'No way. I'm not trained for that.'

'So you don't really trust yourself, then,' I replied. 'You don't believe in yourself.'

In truth, he hadn't overcome anything. He'd put his life entirely in someone else's hands. He had zero control or influence over the jump. If the instructor's parachute had malfunctioned, this guy wouldn't have been able to take control himself. Sure, he might have taken one or two layers off that fear by committing to the skydive in the first place, but he wasn't getting anything out of the action phase of the commitment, so he hadn't stripped it right back. And he definitely hadn't eliminated that fear, whatever he might have told himself.

In order to overcome that fear, you have to be in full control after the initial commitment phase. This guy could have jumped out of a plane a hundred times, but he wasn't accountable for what happened next. He wasn't giving himself the chance to take charge.

The hard truth is, you've got to carry that weight yourself. Put your life in your own hands. Be in control. That is the way to gain self-belief. To realise, 'Yes, I am capable. I can do this. I trust in this process. I trust the equipment. I trust in myself.'

It's a similar thing with bungee jumping. When you do a jump, you're beginning with a commitment to action, because you're in charge of jumping off the launch platform. That's a positive. But the moment you begin the freefall you're not actioning anything. It's not in your hands anymore. The rope is doing all the work for you, and if you've got a fear of heights, you probably had your eyes closed during the descent. You might have conquered your fear of standing at a great height, or stepping off the pad, but you won't overcome that fear until you own the action from start to finish. In both cases, you'd be better off abseiling down the side of a cliff.

Abseiling is a great test of mental resilience. Once you're

over the edge, you still have to be in full control of your mind and body on the way down. Let go of the rope in your hands, and you'll whoosh down the side of the cliff, hit the ground at speed and either severely injure yourself or die. You have to make a positive commitment to action *during the whole phase of the descent*. That allows you to harness that fear, to take control of it. When you reach the bottom, you're going to benefit from that massively. You'll realise that you are capable. Self-belief will kick in.

Self-belief is about being able to trust in yourself during the action stage of a commitment. That means learning to distinguish between actions that you control versus actions that you don't control.

When I was training in 9 Parachute Squadron, we'd start off by practising how to drop, using a low-level parachute (LLP), by steering and pulling on the rigging lines. Then we progressed on to our landing drills, jumping down from a height of twenty metres while attached to a rope rigged up to a fan-assisted harness. This is supposed to bring you down at the speed of a parachute, so you're prepared for how to land correctly, but it's nothing like the real thing.

I didn't really take full control of the action until I was chucked out of the back of a Skyvan for the first time.

I was bricking it on that first jump. Had my eyes closed, which is a big no-no. During your descent you're taught to count off in your head: 'One thousand, two thousand, three thousand . . .' Once you hit 'eight thousand' you're supposed to look up, check the canopy. Make sure it's fully opened. I didn't do any of this stuff. I just felt the canopy dragging me around. The counting didn't even come into play.

SELF-BELIEF IS
ABOUT BEING
ABLE TO TRUST IN
YOURSELF DURING
THE ACTION STAGE
OF A COMMITMENT.
THAT MEANS
LEARNING TO
DISTINGUISH
BETWEEN ACTIONS
THAT YOU CONTROL
VERSUS ACTIONS
THAT YOU DON'T
CONTROL.

But with every jump – with every commitment to take full charge of that action – I learned a bit more about myself. And I got better.

Of course, some things will be outside your control. That's just life. If you and your muckers are getting mortared by the enemy, out in the open, you won't be able to influence whether the bombs will land on you or not. It's out of your hands.

However, when you seek control of an action that is within your domain, you are always going to learn from it. It doesn't matter whether that action is positive or negative – whether you succeed or fail in that particular process. The important thing is to stay in control of the action at all times. You have to *choose* to maintain control. It's a conscious decision.

Even if you fail at a controlled action, you can still learn from it and rectify your mistake. Then you won't make that mistake on the next attempt. But if you're not in full control, you won't know that. The lesson will go unlearned. You'll make the error of going back to the drawing board.

That's what happens when people don't take complete control of their actions. They think to themselves, 'I can't do this. I've failed at this once already. Therefore, I'm a failure.' But they're only thinking this because they haven't controlled the action from start to finish, so they don't have the tools they need to find a solution. Whereas they might be better off telling themselves, 'If I take charge of this action, if I'm prepared to control it throughout this phase, I'm going to learn from it.'

Always seek to control the action. Own it. Don't let someone else take control of the dive for you.

LESSON 22

EMBRACE THE POSITIVE MINDSET

I've always tried to lead by example. That's equally true when we're filming *SAS Australia*. It might seem like a small thing, but it's important to show the recruits that what we're asking of them isn't impossible. That it really can be done.

On the very first season of the show, we were filming around the Snowy Mountains in New South Wales. We had the recruits doing various drills: ice-axe drills, which involve digging your ice axe into the ground when you slip, and crevasse drills. The latter is used when the person you're attached to falls into a crevasse (when you're operating in an Arctic or mountain environment, you're tied to someone else by means of a rope). When that happens, you have to immediately drop to the ground and dig in your heels, using your crampons to stop yourself from being dragged down into the crevasse as well. Then you have to anchor to a safety point and create a haulage system to pull your mate out.

All of this is based on UK Arctic warfare training. It's what makes the Royal Marine Commandos an elite fighting force:

unlike the Paras or other conventional forces, the Marines are trained to operate in every kind of environment.

As we were walking through this area I noticed a nearby lake. 'That's the perfect place to do a backwards dive exercise,' I said, pointing to it. 'We can get a chopper in, put it over the middle of the lake, get everyone to backwards dive into the water and swim to the shore.'

Someone pointed out that the lakes surrounding the Snowy Mountains are made of glacier water. The area gets very cold in the winter, the mountains are capped with snow, temperatures can drop to between minus ten and twenty degrees Celsius.

'Just how cold is that lake?' I enquired.

'Eight degrees,' came the reply.

'Great,' I said. 'That's fine.'

The producer stared at me. 'Ant, are you sure?'

'One hundred per cent, mate,' I said. 'I want it done in that lake.'

We didn't bother with a rehearsal, which was my decision. But when the day of the filming arrived people were telling me, 'Ant, it's eight bloody degrees, for Christ's sake. You'll need to come in a bit closer to the shore. You can't dive in from two hundred metres away, it's too far. You're going to freeze.'

I didn't take any notice. My mistake.

With the recruits looking on I climbed into the helicopter and told the pilot to take us over the lake. Once we were at the midway point I moved towards the edge of the cabin and backwards dived into the water.

The cold shock hit me as soon as I broke the surface. The water was viciously cold. In my eagerness to set the example

I'd forgotten what eight degrees feels like. I came up to the surface gasping for air, the cold stabbing at my skin. I told myself to calm down. Then I looked up towards the shoreline. I could just about make out the recruits and the crew. They looked as small as pins.

'Jesus,' I thought. 'I'm bloody miles away.'

I started to swim. Within a very short time my body began to seize up. I was in agony, I had severe muscle cramps. I knew then I was in serious trouble.

I came very, very close to panicking and giving up. At any point I could have looked over to the rescue jet ski moving alongside me and signalled to them to bring me in. That's all it would have taken. Then the rescue team would have thrown me the safety rope, and I could have dragged myself onto the emergency lifeboard shackled to the stern. The pain would have been at an end. But my mind refused to accept that option.

'The recruits are watching me,' I thought. 'I can't do that. I've got to swim to that shore.'

So I kept going. Kept telling myself, 'I know my body. I know the pain. I've been through worse than this. I've been here before.'

It took me an eternity to swim towards that shoreline. When I finally dragged myself out of the water I was in a really bad state. I had been in the lake for several minutes; my fingers were tightening up, my jaw was beginning to lock.

The recruits had their backs to me, so I started running up and down the beach in a frantic effort to warm up my body. Then I told the recruits to turn round.

'Pay attention,' I said as I began the briefing. 'You've seen the demonstration, I'm going to tell you this once and once only. Keep your arms tight. Lean back. Don't screw this up. First recruit with me. Let's go.'

I climbed into the helicopter with the first recruit, still wearing my soaking wet clothes. 'We're going to need to reduce the distance,' I told the pilot. 'Drop them fifty metres from the shore. If you drop this lot where you dropped me, some of them are going to struggle. They could get seriously injured. Maybe even drown.'

We set off on the first run. I usually like to stay in my wet clothes in that kind of situation – I like to feel the cold, the pain. But on this occasion, it was a really bad idea. Because I was coming down with hypothermia.

I recognised the signs. Hypothermia is a very different type of pain from just being really cold. I was shivering badly; my mind was clouded and confused. I could hardly remember throwing the first five or six recruits out of the chopper. Although I knew my body well enough to understand what was happening, I was determined not to give in.

'This is only the beginning of the course,' I reminded myself. 'I've got twenty recruits to get through. I'm not going to stop. I'll have to collapse before anyone can stop me from seeing this through.'

Through sheer persistence, I managed to get through the worst of it. After the fifth or sixth recruit, I started to recover. My body temperature began to regulate. The hypothermia faded. The pain gradually subsided. For the last ten recruits, I was fully back in the game. The power of positivity pulled me through that pain.

The moment you tell yourself, 'I'm gone, I can't do this,' the moment you let that negative thought penetrate your mind, then you've lost. You're giving your mind permission to surrender power. Giving your physical self the psychological affirmation it needs to shut down. To quit.

NEVER, EVER, UNDERESTIMATE THE POWER OF POSITIVE THINKING.

If you're going to resist this – to fight against it – you need to eliminate any sliver of negativity from your mind.

Never, ever, underestimate the power of positive thinking.

Whatever the situation – whether you're learning to walk again after a serious injury, or if you're afraid of crowds – the power of the positive mindset is strong enough to drag your body through any negative situation you might face. Positivity is what got me through that swim. It's what pulled me through when I was coming down with hypothermia. It's what gets you through the toughest moments.

When you read about people who've fought off sharks, they'll often say that during the attack they kept telling themselves, 'I want to survive, I want to survive,' even after their legs had been bitten off. That's a positive mindset in a nutshell.

But if someone in that situation thinks to themselves, 'Well, I'm screwed now, there's no way out,' then they're definitely going to struggle. You're not going to escape the Great White that's trying to kill you. This is also true in your daily life: a growing number of studies have demonstrated that there's a link between a positive mindset and physical health. People with a positive outlook are more likely to have healthier immune systems, better cardiovascular systems, lower blood pressure. They tend to live longer.

Of course, that doesn't mean you should embrace delusion. That's a dangerous mindset and must be avoided at all costs. But when you put positivity into practice, when you truly believe in something, it almost blinds you to everything else. It drowns out the other noise, and lets you see what you're truly capable of. It's the most powerful weapon in your arsenal – so use it.

ALEXANDER THE GREAT VERSUS THE PERSIANS

In 331 BC, Alexander the Great and his troops were camped a short distance from the Persian army, at a place called Gaugamela, about five hundred kilometres north of Babylon.

The Macedonians were heavily outnumbered at Gaugamela. Alexander had 47,000 soldiers under his command. Facing him was a Persian force of at least 100,000 men, led by Darius III, including archers, war elephants, scythed chariots and the 'Immortals', the hardcore Persian elite infantry. They also had as many as 10,000 Greek mercenaries. Most people, faced with these odds, would have panicked or withdrawn. But Alexander was not most people.

When Alexander's generals saw the size of the force drawn up against them, they approached the king and suggested attacking at night. Not only would this maintain the element of surprise, they said, but fighting in the dark would also give their men a psychological boost because they wouldn't see the size of the enemy force they were fighting against.

Alexander rejected his generals' plan. He said he had no intention of stealing his victory. Fighting by night, in a time before the invention of NVGs (Night Vision Goggles), was very risky. It's hard to coordinate an army in the darkness, meaning confusion and panic can quickly set in and, ultimately, resulting in defeat. They would be better off attacking in daylight, Alexander argued. That way, when the Persians were soundly beaten, they would have no excuses to fight on. Their confidence would be broken: they would realise that it was pointless to keep on resisting the might of the Macedonian army.

This is where the genius of Alexander is on full display. Of course he was supremely arrogant, but his arrogance was built on the foundations of confidence in himself and his men. He knew that a night attack was a terrible idea from a tactical point of view; but he also understood that the Persians would be *expecting* a night attack, because the Macedonians were so heavily outnumbered.

As a result, the Persian troops had to stand in their formations all night. Instead of enjoying a nice warm meal and getting some much-needed sleep, they would be physically drained the next day. Psychologically their heads wouldn't be in the right place either: waiting in the dark for an attack that might come at any moment would shred their nerves and put them at a disadvantage the next day. This would give Alexander's men a small but decisive edge in the coming fight.

Early the next morning, Alexander's officers went to see their king and were amazed to discover that Alexander was still asleep. This is another example of his positive mindset. He wasn't lying awake all night, tossing and turning with anxiety, worrying about whether he might win the next day.

You can't fake this stuff: you can only get that when you're living and breathing positivity.

After a while one of his generals plucked up the courage to enter Alexander's tent and wake him up. When he asked Alexander how he could oversleep when he was about to fight his most important battle, Alexander was said to have smiled and explained that they were already victorious because they had finally got what they wanted. After wandering about the country, chasing Darius and his men, Alexander went on, they now had the chance to settle things once and for all.

Alexander had unshakeable confidence in his men and his own abilities. This wasn't delusion: he knew from previous scraps that the Persian forces were no match for his heavy infantry and his mobile cavalry. He truly believed they would win – that there was no option but to win. That positivity and self-belief transmitted itself to the men under his command. And this proved invaluable in the fighting that followed.

Darius, the Persian king, had levelled the ground at the point where he expected the battle to be fought so he could deploy his chariots and cavalry. Alexander, commanding a section of cavalry on the Macedonian right, pushed his men further and further to the right flank, drawing the Persian horsemen towards him. Darius hesitated to attack – he'd fallen for the same trick before and knew what to expect – but when he saw that Alexander and his cavalry had almost reached the limits of the levelled ground, he ordered his heavily armoured horsemen to move forward.

At some point during the struggle Alexander forced a gap in the enemy line. Now he scented blood. He immediately charged through the opening with his cavalry and made straight for King Darius himself. Although the Persians fought hard, Darius panicked and fled on horseback. Some of his troops retreated; many others were cut down before they could escape.

It was then that a message reached Alexander informing him that his left flank was at risk of being wiped out. Alexander grudgingly called off his pursuit of the Persian king and rushed to help out his left flank. Eventually the Macedonians emerged victorious. Darius was later arrested by his own men, taken prisoner and killed.

At every stage of the battle, Alexander had maintained total belief in both himself and his ability to smash his opponent. He refused to let negative thoughts creep into his mind. He approached the challenge confident in his chances. The result was an astonishing victory that destroyed the superpower of the Persian empire.

DON'T BE AFRAID TO BREAK THE RULES

Sometimes, to get the job done, you need to be ready to break a few rules.

History is full of examples of great commanders who were more than willing to go against the grain when the situation called for it.

Iphicrates was one of the outstanding soldiers of ancient Greece. During his career he transformed the Athenian army. He did away with the large shields and chain-mail body armour traditionally favoured by the infantry and encouraged them to fight as mobile infantry, equipping them with lighter shields and linen armour, lowering the weight they had to carry with them. He also ditched the short swords and spears, replacing them with longer versions. Iphicrates drilled his men hard, training them in every conceivable situation they might face from ambushes to civilian revolt.

Over time, Iphicrates's men gained a reputation as the toughest and most disciplined warriors in all of Greece.

Shaka, chief of the Zulus, was also a rule-breaker, as well as being a complete madman. One of his big ideas was to change the Zulu warrior's style of fighting. Instead of lobbing spears at their enemies from a distance, Shaka realised they could do a lot more damage by using stabbing spears at close-range. He introduced a shorter spear called the Iklwa, reportedly named after the sucking noise it made when tearing it free from human flesh.

Shaka also came up with a trademark formation called the 'Bullhorn', featuring a central force ('the chest') flanked by a pair of 'horns' on both sides, often concealed from the enemy until the last possible moment, plus a fourth set of veteran blokes in reserve. The idea in battle was to use the chest to get to grips with the enemy, pinning them in place while the horns swept round to attack from the flanks. When it worked, it was utterly devastating.

Whatever the era, the lesson is always the same: new challenges have to be met with new solutions. To solve problems, sometimes you have to be willing to ditch the old ways of thinking. Be a rule-breaker.

'When another person asked why the Spartans, in their wars, ventured boldly into danger, he said, "Because we train ourselves to have regard for life and not, like others, to be timid about it."'

*Anaxandridas, Agiad King of
Sparta, circa 560–520 BC*

BE BOLD

Whenever I'm tackling something new, I'll take the same approach. I'll get a general idea of what the task involves, enough to grasp the overall picture, but I won't do a ton of homework beforehand. Instead, I'll go in with what I call *positive naïveté*.

Boldness isn't the same as being reckless. Don't confuse the two. Boldness is about being naïve about a challenge in a positive way. Having the confidence in yourself and in your own capabilities to solve any problems you might encounter without overthinking them before you begin.

When you approach a task boldly – with that element of positive naïveté – you're trusting in yourself. You're demonstrating total belief in your ability to come up with a solution no matter what. And when you're confronted by something unexpected, you're so naïve about it that you're forced to face it there and then.

Overanalysing a task beforehand encourages negativity to the extent that it will overpower your positive mindset. If you approach a challenge anticipating all the potential scenarios and hurdles you might face in advance, you're giving yourself too many options. You're opening the door to doubt and surrender.

A good example of this is when we're told, 'Make sure you plan for the worst-case scenario.' Which is nonsense. If you took that mindset and applied it to your daily life, you'd be walking on eggshells the whole time.

I never plan for worst-case scenarios. I know what I need to do if things go wrong, generally speaking, but in the moment I might respond completely differently. I might choose to tackle the problem another way. Come at it from another direction. That's a healthier attitude than planning in detail for every possible catastrophe that might befall you in life.

I'm an extremely confident person, but part of that confidence comes from not being afraid of failing or screwing up. Accepting that it's part of my existence. That it will be present in my life every day until the day I die.

Positive naïveté is a powerful weapon in anyone's toolbox. It enables you to tackle challenges with excitement rather than trepidation.

I employed this mentality all the time as a soldier. Whenever I went into combat, I didn't try to anticipate every possible eventuality before my boots hit the ground. I didn't sweat the details. I knew the broad outlines of the job, what I might be coming up against, but if I encountered an IED or ran into a heavy firefight, I had the confidence to tell myself, 'I'll deal with that in the moment, right there and then.'

I allowed myself to be positively naïve.

Positive naïveté allows you to solve problems much faster and more efficiently. By telling your mind, 'I'm going to overcome this, I'm going to solve this problem' you're giving yourself only one option. Instead of second-guessing what might happen, you're placing absolute faith in yourself. You're gambling on yourself. On your ability to problem-solve in real-time.

When you have the boldness to commit, to be positively naïve in your approach, you'll be astonished at what you can achieve.

If you're faced with an unfamiliar task at work, or you're tackling a new sport, don't overanalyse before you begin. That will only stop you from attempting the challenge. Be bold and go for it.

'Do not repeat the tactics which have gained you one victory, but let your methods be regulated by the infinite variety of circumstance.'

Sun Tzu, The Art of War, Chapter 6.28

LESSON 25

BE THE GOOD SOLDIER

Being a good soldier means having the ability to make split-second decisions knowing in your heart of hearts that you're making those decisions from a place of goodness. When you do that, you'll be able to live with yourself afterwards.

I always knew that I was a good solider. Because my decision-making came from a good place. From a good man. A good heart. I wasn't interested in going around and whacking people just for the sake of it.

We're not programmed to kill one another. That's why militaries invest huge amounts of time and money in training soldiers to go to war. Because we have to be *conditioned* to fight.

Soldiers know it's not about how many targets you kill. We're not interested in killing people for the sake of it. We have moral values. We seek to do good in the world. And so should you.

I'm not a practising Catholic, but there's a verse from the

Bible that has always stayed with me. Romans 12, Verse 21: 'Do not be overcome by evil but overcome evil with good.'

Have good intentions in whatever you do. That might sound corny, but it's easy to forget that lesson in today's world. There are plenty of people in all walks of society who aspire to be bullies with weapons. Don't be one of them. Make your decisions based on good intentions.

- Stay focused. Don't let frustration win. Don't let your opponent see the chink in your armour.

- Self-doubt is your enemy. Never carry it into the sports arena or the job interview. At the first sign of it, get rid. Only good things can come from bringing a positive mindset to your work or craft.

- Avoid indecision. Make a decision. Remind yourself that doing something is always better than doing nothing. Accept that you'll make mistakes sometimes, but if you felt that the decision you took was the right one at the time, then you'll be able to live with the consequences. And if it's the wrong one, then you'll have the chance to learn from the experience – to make a better decision next time round.

- Remember that emotional intelligence is a core part of the successful soldier, just as it's important in business or sports or your personal life. Don't shut your emotions away in the armoury. Have the courage to take them out and analyse them. Understand them. When you know where an emotion has come from and why, then you'll be able to make it work for you instead of working against you.

- Take control of your actions. Be in control of your own skydive.

- Use the power of the positive mindset. Apply that to everything you do in life. Positivity is what will drag you through when you're in a freezing cold lake and struggling to reach the shore.

- Know when to break the rules – and don't be afraid to do it when necessary.

- Embrace the concept of positive naïveté. Be bold in your commitments to action.

- Always aspire to be the good soldier. When you do good, you'll learn to be good. Don't be a bully with a weapon. Understand the importance of empathy. Make your decisions from a place of pureness.

PART FOUR

DISASTER AND ADVERSITY

LESSON 26

EMBRACE FAILURE

Things rarely go according to plan. That's especially true in the military. There's a seed of truth to that old saying that no plan survives contact with the enemy.

Failure is a fact of life. We can't abolish it, any more than we can get rid of death, or poverty, or war. But in today's world, failure is considered a dirty word. People don't want to go near it. Which means that they become afraid of committing to action in the first place, because of the fear of failing that modern society has engrained in us.

In the military, I knew some guys who were top soldiers, at the absolute peak of their profession, but they wouldn't dare attempt Selection. They were scared of doing it, because the failure rate is staggeringly high. These lads were the kings of the castles in their own units, but they were afraid of not making it through. They didn't want to risk being part of the ninety-five per cent who failed military training, because they'd have to go back to their little castle in the Royal Marines or the Paras, thinking of themselves as failures. I had no doubt that some of these guys would have passed Selection if they had the courage to commit to their process. But the fear of failure was too strong.

It stopped them from achieving their goal.

Before you can achieve anything in life, you need to learn to embrace failure. Tell yourself, 'I have failed every day of my life. I will continue to fail every day until the day I die.' Failure is universal, and it's happening all the time: it's as much a part of our daily existence as breathing. Whether it's failing an exam, or being late for a meeting, or failing a mission in the field, it's always going to be there. So it's pointless trying to banish it from your life.

BEFORE YOU CAN ACHIEVE ANYTHING IN LIFE, YOU NEED TO LEARN TO EMBRACE FAILURE.

Fear of failure stops people in their tracks. They become incapable of making decisions because they're petrified of messing up. They end up living in the Void. They go through life on autopilot, driven by fear and anxiety, scared to be labelled a failure. The negative mindset starts to dominate. Whenever a task becomes difficult or stressful, they won't be able to see it through. So they abandon the challenge. They hold up their hands and say, 'I can't do this, it's too hard.' And in their minds, they become the very thing they fear the most: *a failure.*

Here's the truth. Failure can either work for you, or against you. If you're not embracing failure, it's going to stop you from actioning or committing to something. When you don't commit, you don't learn. When you're not learning, you're not able to grow.

If you don't grow, you'll never realise what you are really capable of, and you'll be surrendering the possibility of becoming a better version of yourself.

Once you start embracing failure, however, you learn how to make it work for you. You start to see that there's this huge reward side to failure. You'll realise that when you commit – when you're no longer afraid to fail – the task will excite you instead of overwhelming you.

Reaching your goal won't be easy, of course: you'll need to work hard, make sacrifices, accept that the path might involve detours along the way, deal with positive stress and pressure and all the other things that are necessary before you can achieve anything of value. But if you're prepared to go down that route, if you're prepared to graft, there's a huge reward lying in wait for you.

If you don't embrace failure, it will limit your potential as an individual. You'll look at everything in a negative light. The task will look too overwhelming. Instead of getting excited by it, you'll talk yourself out of attempting it, and you'll end up not committing at all. You won't achieve what you want because you won't even set out in the first place.

We have a habit of looking at everything we do through the prism of possible failure. 'What if I fail? What if I don't get this right?' I don't care who you are or what you've achieved, that fear of failing is always going to be there.

Ignoring it – hoping it goes away – never works. The moment you try to do that, you're ignoring ten or twenty per cent of your mindset. Therefore, you're only going to function at eighty or ninety per cent of your potential capability.

People tend to get caught in the trap of thinking, 'If I don't succeed at this task, I'm going to become a *failure*.' They put themselves in a negative mindset before they've even started. Then it doesn't work, and they tell themselves, 'I'm a failure.' It confirms the idea they've already planted in their heads. The next time they're faced with a challenge, they won't even commit to attempt it. They'll palm it off on someone else.

The first step towards embracing failure is to accept that it's not going anywhere. Understand that, whether you like it or not, failure is going to be present in your life every day, emotionally, physically and psychologically.

Once you accept that, you'll realise that failure – and the fear of failure – is just another part of you. A part of the complex whole. And like any other part of you, it's impossible to function properly without it.

Then you can begin to face that failure head on. You'll gain the strength to say to yourself, 'Let's do this. I'm going to commit to this and see where it takes me.' It takes real courage to do that.

Don't let fear of failure stop you from achieving your goals. Instead, look it in the eye. Embrace failure, acknowledge it and make it work for you, and you'll be able to commit to action instead of avoiding it.

'If you know the enemy and you know yourself, you need not fear the result of a hundred battles. If you know yourself but not the enemy, for every victory gained you will also suffer a defeat. If you know neither the enemy nor yourself, you will succumb in every battle.'

Sun Tzu, The Art of War, Chapter 3.18

LESSON 27

SURVIVE HARDSHIP

The best lessons in life are the hardest ones, the ones that wound you the deepest. That taste the bitterest.

When my father passed away, he left me the biggest gift I could have ever asked for in life.

He gave me my mindset.

I was five years old when he died. In the blink of an eye, my whole life was turned upside down. Everything changed. A new man came into our lives. When I was nine, we upped sticks and moved to a rural area not far from Saint-Lô in Normandy. I was enrolled in the local Catholic school. This was a hugely confusing time for me: I was in a strange environment, no one spoke any English and most of all I missed my dad.

We had a row of fir trees at the back of our garden, bordering a farmer's field. I used to dig a hole under the trees, crawl into the hedge. Make myself a little den. That place became a sort of refuge for me. I remember one day running into the den and breaking down in tears. I had this terrible feeling of being completely overwhelmed. I started having this conversation inside my head.

'Why am I feeling like this?' I asked myself. 'Well, lots of reasons. I miss Dad. I'm in a new school. I can't speak the language.'

Without realising it, I was starting to self-reflect. Processing my feelings.

As soon as I realised that, I felt better. I understood why I was feeling the way I did. I'd unpacked those emotions. Of course I was sad and lonely and confused. Because I missed my dad. Anyone else would feel exactly the same in that situation. That was a completely normal reaction.

Instead of giving in to panic or despair, I was rationalising.

I couldn't bring my father back, nothing could change that, but I *could* think positively about him. Remind myself that he's looking down on me, that he was a positive person, so maybe I should copy him. Follow his example and be positive myself. Things would be very hard, but I'd start to feel a bit better if I focused on other things and tried to keep my mind occupied. I could knuckle down to learn the language, for example. Focus on making my dad proud.

Within a few months, I was fluent in French. That helped hugely with life at school. The sense of achievement gave me self-belief.

I carried this mindset through into my military career. This ability to rationalise things whenever I was going through a tough moment or facing some unforeseen difficulty.

I'd ask myself, 'Why did I freeze at that door back there? Because I was scared. Okay. Why was I scared? Because bullets were flying through that door. Well, that's perfectly reasonable. That's a natural reaction. Nine times out of ten, in that situation, I'll turn flight into fight, but every so often that urge to take flight will come back into the equation. No need to get angry or upset about it. It is what it is.'

Through having that conversation with myself, by rationalising what seemed to be irrational at first glance, I'd know what to do. 'Okay, acknowledge your reaction. Accept that you're human. Take a deep breath. Slow things down. Try and approach it again. Be more methodical this time. Let's take it from there.'

This goes back to being honest with yourself. If you're able to sit down and reflect honestly on your situation, without falling into the trap of overanalysing or overthinking, that will free you as an individual.

Whether it's on the battleground or in the workplace, when you overthink, you'll start to see things that aren't there. You'll end up solving problems that don't really exist anywhere except inside your own head. You're trying to control things that by their very nature are *uncontrollable*. That, in turn, will induce anxiety and stress. You'll overcompensate and second-guess. Eventually that's going to eat you up. You'll enter a negative spiral. You'll become angry and start blaming yourself. Your mind becomes fixated on could-haves and should-haves, wishing that things had gone differently.

But that's a destructive conversation. No good can come of it. When you start thinking like that, you're only digging deeper into a hole of unreality until it becomes the norm. You'll end up living in an overanalysed world that takes up all of your time, all of your attention, all of your thought processes. It will consume you and ultimately ruin your life. You'll end up pushing yourself away from people because you're not living in reality.

When you're faced with hardship, think rationally. Have that conversation inside your head. Understand why you're feeling the way you are. Don't overthink the situation. Instead of giving in to despair, ask yourself, 'How am I going to get through this? How am I going to cope? How am I going to overcome this situation?'

In those moments when life becomes extremely difficult, whether you've been made redundant at your company or you've been in a relationship that has irrevocably broken down, hold yourself accountable, re-prioritise, take hold of your responsibilities. And most of all learn from your experiences. Hardship is a powerful learning tool – if you know how to use it.

LESSON 28

BE HONEST

When I walked through the door of my local Job Centre, I was at a real low-point in my life.

I'd left the army several months earlier. I loved life in the military, but I was tired of the attitude of some of the other lads. I felt, rightly or wrongly, that I was better than them. Consequently, I'd isolated myself from the other lads. By then I knew that the Parachute Squadron wasn't for me. I'd made up my mind to join the Royal Marines, but the process was more straightforward if I left the army and reapplied. So that's what I did.

I had some time between leaving and reapplying, so I decided to get a job. Figured I could easily land something short-term. But after two months, things weren't looking good. I still hadn't found any work, and to make matters worse I'd got into a bit of trouble. A stupid little scrap in town. That screwed my plans for the Royal Marines because I couldn't reapply until the charges had been dropped. I found myself in limbo.

Which was why I found myself down the Job Centre one morning, clutching my little red book.

Back then, when you left the military, you were given a red book containing all your service credentials. Mine had my Parachute Training, Best Recruit, Best PT and so on.

As soon as I stepped inside, one of the advisors caught sight of me. Young bloke. He recognised the book I was carrying. Nodded at it. 'Are you ex-military, mate?' he asked. 'Come over here. Have a seat.'

I walked over to his desk. Sat down. Handed him my book. The advisor started flicking through the pages and saying offhandedly, 'Yeah, we get loads of these books coming through here. Let's see what job we can find you.'

He kept on flicking through the pages. After a while he looked up at me. 'Why did you leave the military?' he asked.

I started to explain my reasons.

'Mate,' the advisor went on, 'look, I've seen hundreds of these books. Literally hundreds of them have passed my desk, and you've got some of the best credentials I've ever seen.'

He closed the book. Passed it back to me.

'Go back into that space,' he added.

Then he got up and walked off. Didn't look for a job for me. Didn't even go through my situation with me. I sat there for a few moments feeling a bit confused and embarrassed. Then I rose to my feet, grabbed my book and walked out of the Job Centre, as jobless as I had been when I'd strolled inside.

For some reason I decided to sit on the front steps. I looked across to my right. A dishevelled old geezer sat a few paces away, clutching a can of cheap lager. He had a couple of stained teeth; his breath reeked of fags. I had £1.37 in my pocket, skint as you could possibly be.

'Christ, I'm no better than this sad bastard,' I thought.

That was a rude awakening.

I asked myself a painful question. 'Why are you sitting on these steps, jobless and broke?'

For the first time in my life, I was unsparingly honest with myself. I took no prisoners. Started ripping myself apart.

'You're here,' I realised, 'because you're big-headed. Everyone got promoted over you because you thought you were better than them. You didn't want to mix, you isolated yourself. You weren't a team player. You got your best recruit, best PT and rested on your laurels when you should have been pushing on.'

I came to a realisation about my time in the Parachute Squadron. I hadn't been focused on being the best version of me. I had been too focused on trying to be the best at everything.

It might sound strange, but I felt so refreshed and so good about being honest with myself, even though this had happened at one of the lowest moments in my life. I saw that I had enjoyed a gleaming start to my military career, but through my own mistakes I'd messed everything up.

That moment of honesty allowed me to see, with complete clarity, what I needed to do to get back into that space. I understood that I needed to calm my ego down. I had to become a team player. Be the best version of me. Make sure I kept growing, that I didn't get comfortable. Not make the mistake of thinking I'm the best in my unit simply because I've smashed a few exercises.

When I broke it down in that way, it felt like an epiphany. It gave me the jolt I needed to help me clean up my act.

The charges against me were eventually dropped and I was free to join the Royal Marines. I went in there with renewed determination, smashed the early exercises and was awarded the King's Badge, which is given to the recruit who accumulates the most points during Commando Training.*

That was a telling moment in my Royal Marines career. It took me back to the mistakes I'd made in the Parachute Squadron. I was determined not to repeat them again.

'Get to your unit and keep your momentum going,' I reminded myself. 'You're King's Badge now, but that's nothing. When you make it to your unit, don't just rest on your green beret or your King's Badge. Go and do your courses. Keep working.'

This time, I kept my momentum up.

Being honest is not something you only need to do once. You need to practise it continuously throughout your life. When you start being honest with yourself, you'll often discover that the problem or the solution is right there in front of you. It's probably been there the whole time, you just weren't honest enough to acknowledge or recognise it. Or you were lying to yourself about the reality of your situation.

A lot of people lie to themselves. Therefore they *live a lie*. That can be incredibly damaging in the long run because you can't lie to yourself. You're going to find it very hard to live with those lies, because you can't forget or ignore what you know deep down to be true.

Being honest with yourself will change you as an individual. It is an act of courage. It's one of the hardest things you will ever do. But the more you do it, the easier it becomes.

---

* The King's Badge dates back to 1918, during the reign of King George V, when the award was first given to the top Royal Marine recruit in the senior squad, otherwise known as the 'King's Squad'.

And there are only positives to be gleaned from being fully honest with yourself.

Perhaps you're not totally honest about your personality traits. Maybe there's two or three per cent of your character that you don't like or you're ashamed of, or you try to hide from other people. Maybe you have an arrogant streak. But by concealing or denying it you're allowing other people to bring it to the forefront. They'll turn the spotlight on that lie. 'John is arrogant,' they'll say. That will engulf the other ninety-eight or ninety-seven per cent of who you are, because you'll be telling yourself, 'Shit, they've sussed me out.' Other people will amplify the volume of your lies until they completely dominate you.

Honesty is vital in the military. People talk about being 'brutally honest' but in the military there's no such thing. There's either honesty or dishonesty. If you want to achieve at a high level you need to be direct and open in your feedback. You need to have direct conversations about solving problems.

Society encourages us to tiptoe around stuff rather than face it head-on. If you haven't performed well at your job, you'll know that your efforts weren't up to scratch. But a colleague might try to reassure you and say, 'Don't worry about it.' Because they're afraid of upsetting you. Then you automatically think, 'Yeah, it *was* okay.' You unconsciously lower your standards. It's a human instinct. If someone praises you for doing a mediocre job, what's the motivation for you to do better the next time round?

The military mindset is completely different. We are trained to be honest with one another because there are real-world consequences to every decision we take. If we screw up, we're going to have blood on our hands.

Instead of getting shirty when someone calls us out, we're thinking, 'I'm glad you mentioned that I was below the level back there, mate. I know where my standards are, you know where my standards are, and I needed to hear that.'

When you're honest with yourself, that has a huge knock-on effect on your honesty towards other people, and the situation at hand.

In the military, that honesty is absolutely essential to mission success. We might be planning a mission and I'll ask my pal, 'What's behind that door?' Whatever they tell me, I'm going to act on that information. That's the level of responsibility you have.

No one questioned what we had seen or heard. But we had to be *sure*. It's no good us saying, 'It could have been this,' or, 'I might have seen that.' Whatever I said would get acted on as verified information. A tiny detail might be absolutely consequential in ways you can't always easily predict. Make a mistake, and it could result in innocent people being killed down the line.

We had to be comfortable with that level of responsibility. And we were. Because we were honest with ourselves and each other.

Be courageously honest in your life. Have the courage to face yourself and ask the very hard questions. If you are not honest with yourself, or with the progress you want to make, then you can easily become complacent and give up on your goals. Honesty creates accountability. When you practise honesty of self, you'll begin to be outwardly honest as well. That will free you as an individual.

LESSON 29

DON'T SWITCH OFF

It was the first phase of Selection.

I was going across some hard terrain, head down, weight on my back. Totally exhausted. Hanging out of my arse. Then the clag swooped in. Low cloud, damp and grey, shrouding the landscape, screwing my visibility. I couldn't see any further than the tip of my nose.

Eventually the clag began to clear. Then the realisation hit me: I was lost. I didn't have a clue where I was. I started to think I was going to fail. 'That's me done, I'm going to be sent back to my unit.'

As soon as that thought started creeping into my mind, I shut the door on it. I told myself I wasn't going to fail, no matter what. I'd rather die.

Eventually I understood what had happened. When that clag had descended over the landscape I'd veered off the route. In my fatigued state I'd switched off for a moment, and paid the price. But I didn't dwell on my mistake. Instead, I concentrated on fixing it. So I readjusted, figured out where I was on the map. Re-orientated myself and got back on the correct bearing.

That was a great lesson for me. It made me realise that I could never afford to switch off. On a mission, the consequences could be fatal.

When you're doing a task, make sure you don't switch off. Even if it's just for a split-second. Make that mistake, and you'll end up lost in your own personal clag.

LESSON 30

DEAL WITH CATASTROPHE

When things go badly wrong, the mission goes out of the window. The mission is no longer about the target, or whatever it may be. The mission becomes helping each other to get through.

Teamwork, at its most fundamental level, is about coming together as a team when the shit hits the fan. It means looking each other in the eye and letting your muckers know that we're all in this together. That we're going to get out of it together. When our backs are against the wall and the enemy is moving towards us, there's only one way out. That's through teamwork.

A team that is committed and dedicated to each other will jointly find a solution to problems. By looking towards your teammates, you'll bring together different points of view. Different perspectives, different ways of thinking and breaking things down. You'll be able to identify the source of the error, establish where you went wrong and find a way to get around or solve the crisis.

The one thing you should *never* do is take it personally.

There's a temptation, in the military, for some guys to beat themselves up when tragedy strikes. If your mate gets blown up by an IED, or the guy in front of you is killed during a sweep through a compound, it's super-hard not to take that personally.

It becomes easy for soldiers to tell themselves, 'I should have done more,' or to think, 'If I had done that mission differently, my mate might still be alive.' You end up taking things personally, to a very unhealthy degree.

But in truth, war is never personal. The enemy weren't shooting at me because I'm Ant Middleton. They didn't plant an IED thinking, 'I really hope Ant Middleton steps on this thing.' They were just doing it to halt our advance, or slow us down, or send a message. There was nothing personal about it.

Whenever something went terribly wrong, the first thing I would tell the guys is, 'It's not personal.'

The moment you tell yourself, 'Could have, would have, should have,' you're trying to solve problems that don't actually exist. You're creating your own reality. Your mental health will start to deteriorate. It becomes a vicious circle.

No one deliberately goes out to make mistakes. No one goes into a compound and fails to spot an enemy target or a booby trap on purpose. Identifying where you went wrong is never about apportioning blame – or at least it shouldn't be. It's about taking charge of the error. Studying the problem. Finding solutions.

Everyone screws up. It's a fact of life. The more you try, the more you fail. And the more you fail, the more you bounce back; and the more you bounce back, the stronger you become. But when you take things personally, there probably won't be another screw-up because you won't commit or try the challenge again. Or you won't put yourself in a situation where you have to make a decision in the first place. You'll limit your personal growth.

A good team will help each other through trouble. When people make a mistake, they'll often hold their head in their hands and keep the problem inside them. They'll think, 'Oh Christ, I screwed up. This is *my* problem, what am *I* going to do?'

But that's not true. You are always part of a team. Whether that's your muckers in your Troop, your workmates, friends or family, or the people on your sports team. You're never alone.

It's not your problem. It's *our* problem. And we're going to find a way to deal with it together. We'll rethink and re-attack. Together. *As a team.*

When things go wrong at work, avoid playing the blame game with your colleagues. That doesn't solve anything. Instead try to help each other overcome the difficulty or problem.

LESSON 31

GET OUT OF THE TRENCH

I've seen it happen lots of times. People leave the military. They stop being soldiers; they're no longer part of a squadron or Troop. Their purpose has been taken away from them. All of a sudden, no one is telling them that they're the best all the time. That doesn't happen on Civvy Street: you don't get those repeated messages of affirmation. So they struggle.

They end up in the Void.

When your old purpose has gone, there's no point lingering around it, hoping it will come back. Because it won't. You need to find a new purpose in life.

You don't need to work towards a clearly defined purpose to begin that journey. You just have to commit to *something*. You might commit to ten different things and find that none of them are for you – none of them are giving you that sense of purpose. But that's absolutely fine because as long as you're committing, you're still learning about yourself.

Don't stop looking for your purpose. The moment you do that, you're going to get swallowed up.

When you lose all sense of belonging and purpose, you end up in the Void. You'll drift along, instead of aiming for something. And not only that – you find that you're okay with just ticking along, to the point where you're no longer even aware that it's happening.

I call it going through life on autopilot. You're happy in the Void. Happy to drift aimlessly through life. You've turned your mind into a prison.

No one ends up in the Void by accident. Everyone is there for a reason. Being in the Void is always a choice.

Maybe you've failed to achieve a long-cherished goal. Perhaps you've let someone down. Maybe you're lazy, or a bad person, or you didn't put in the work that you know you should have done. Or you might have suffered a trauma and given up on yourself.

When you're in the Void you're in a place where you have no purpose in life and you're okay with that. It's like anything else: practise enough, and you'll become good at it. That works both ways: negatively, as well as positively. When you practise having no purpose, eventually you're going to become *purposeless.*

Once you're in the Void, it's very hard to claw your way out. To get out of the Void you need to find a purpose. And to find a new purpose is a huge challenge for anyone.

Sometimes we don't even know we're in the Void. We screen out the signals our brain is sending us. Or we succumb to outside narratives. Maybe you're told you're having a midlife crisis, when in fact you're really just living in the Void because your job isn't giving you a sense of purpose. Instead of putting it down to middle age, you'd find it more productive if you concentrated your energies on finding a career that gave you real fulfilment.

I see this all the time. People working towards nothing, trapped in the Void. It's sad to see because I genuinely believe that people have so much potential. But no one else can find a purpose for you. It has to come from within yourself. You need to find that purpose. It has to be something that you believe is purposeful enough to work towards.

Don't make the mistake of thinking that materialistic things will give you a sense of purpose, either. They won't. Having enough money to go on a luxury holiday or buy a shiny new SUV isn't going to give you any sense of real fulfilment. Your purpose has got to be meaningful.

THE PEOPLE I TALK TO INSPIRE ME AS MUCH AS I GIVE TO THEM. THAT'S WHAT GIVES ME MY PURPOSE IN LIFE. THEIR INSPIRATION FUELS ME.

Ideally, purpose should be a two-way street. Teams are an excellent example of this. You've got your purpose, you're working towards helping someone on your team, and they're helping you in return. That sense of mutual purpose can be a very powerful thing. If you're feeling good about what you're doing, and you're also receiving that positivity back from the people you're working with, that sense of purpose is going to stay ignited a lot longer than if it had just come from within you.

My purpose, for example, is helping to motivate and inspire people. But just as importantly, it's a two-way thing. The people I talk to inspire me as much as I give to them. That's what gives me my purpose in life. Their inspiration fuels me.

Try to find something that will give you back as much as you give to it.

In a way, being in the Void is like being in a trench. It's cold and wet, stinking and miserable. You might be stuck there for months and never even fire your weapon once. It's an existence of constant frustration and pain.

In the end, life in the trench will become so unbearable you're going to willingly commit to an attack even when it looks doomed to fail. Getting out of that horrible space and possibly dying in the attack will look like a better option than staying put.

You're already suffering in the trench. If you stick your head above the parapet and die, so be it. But it's better than staying where you are.

We are not supposed to be static. We're problem-solving machines with millions of years of evolution behind us. We've dug tunnels across borders and under oceans, constructed bridges over vast expanses of water. We've given ourselves the power of flight. We've developed the ability to send mission probes to distant planets.

The moment you train yourself to stop doing something that we naturally want to do – solving problems, finding a purpose – that's the moment you choose to live in the Void.

Whatever the situation, when you find yourself in the Void, look for the rope to get out. Commit to something. Just don't quit. No matter what happens, don't stop trying to get out of the hole.

LESSON 32

BE THE BLACKSMITH OF YOUR OWN DESTINY

Never let other people define you.

Think of your destiny as being like a sword being forged by a blacksmith. People and situations will forge you along the way. But once that blade has been shaped, hammered, sanded, quenched and tempered, that's not the end of the process. It still needs to be sharpened.

You are going to be shaped by the world around you. That's a given in life. Situations will forge you in ways that are beyond your control. Maybe someone close to you will abuse your trust. Maybe your business will collapse.

These things will mould you. But what you need to do then is to say to yourself, 'I'm going to sharpen that blade.' Give yourself a new line of attack.

If you don't make the effort to file and polish that blade, it's going to be useless as a weapon. You won't be able to use it to your advantage.

Always remember that this is *your* blade. It's unique. No one else can teach you how to utilise it. So make sure you practise with it. Learn about your sword. How to cut with it, how to parry and feint.

Craft your blade. Define yourself. Let no one else define you. Be the blacksmith of your own destiny.

'David offered himself to Saul to fight with Goliath, the Philistine champion, and, to give him courage, Saul armed him with his own weapons; which David rejected as soon as he had them on his back, saying he could make no use of them, and that he wished to meet the enemy with his sling and his knife. In conclusion, the arms of others either fall from your back, or they weigh you down, or they bind you fast.'

Machiavelli, The Prince, Chapter XIII

LESSON 33

YOU DON'T NEED TO BE PERFECT

During my training in the Royal Marines, I set myself the goal of coming top in both my map-reading and skill-at-arms, otherwise known as the live-fire training course. I placed first on map-reading and came second or third on the live-firing, so I missed out on getting my crossed rifles badge for marksmanship. There wasn't much in it – a couple of rounds at the most.

I was gutted at the time, of course. But I still regarded it as a goal I'd achieved. Because I was in the *vicinity of excellence*.

I'd finished in the top three; I was close enough to reflect on my performance and know that I was only a round or two away from coming top of the drill and getting my marksmanship badge. I didn't need to re-attack that goal because in my mind I hadn't failed it. Therefore I wasn't a failure. I knew I was good enough; with a little more practice I might be able to improve my performance. If anything, I was even more motivated to do better when I moved onto the next test.

LIFE IS ABOUT PROGRESSION, NOT PERFECTION. YOU DON'T HAVE TO CLIMB THE PEAK TO ACHIEVE SOMETHING. YOU ONLY NEED TO BE IN CLOSE PROXIMITY TO THAT PEAK.

People often allow themselves to become deflated when they don't reach a specific goal. They hold a perfect picture in their heads of what their goal looks like, and when they don't attain it, they forget about the progression. Instead of beating themselves up because they didn't achieve perfection, they should be thinking, 'Look at the progress I've made to get this far.'

Life is about progression, not perfection. You don't have to climb the peak to achieve something. You only need to be in close proximity to that peak.

In 2017 I was climbing Mount Aconcagua in Argentina, the highest mountain in the Americas. Our team had made it about 16,000 feet up only to find that conditions were dangerously windy nearer to the peak. My pal had an expedition with him, so he decided to turn around because he didn't want to risk their safety. A few people wanted to stay behind, hire a Sherpa to finish the climb, but that wasn't for me.

I didn't need to reach the top of that mountain. I didn't need that validation. I was already in the general vicinity of achievement. Not making it to the peak didn't mean I was any less capable. If the weather had been different, I would have been standing on the summit. I was happy with the progression I'd made on the ascent. That climb eventually led to me summiting Mount Everest and K2, so in a roundabout way it got me where I wanted to be in the end.

I keep my destinations fairly flexible. I make my goals moveable. It's not a fixed thing. It's easy to train your mind to think in the same way. All you need to do is convince yourself that you're near to that goal. Tell yourself, 'It's good enough, I don't need to prove anything, on another day, in different circumstances, I might have finished top.'

Ultimately, all achievements are man-made. Real achievement is in the eye of the beholder.

People tell me that it's an achievement climbing Everest, or passing Selection, but I don't see it that way at all. I don't look at these things as achievements. I look at everything I've been through as a life experience.

The moment you start viewing things through the narrow prism of achievement, you're also opening up the possibility of seeing yourself as a failure if you don't nail that goal.

You don't need to wear that failure. Focus on the progress you've made and the lessons you've learned. Carry that attitude on to your next goal.

When you approach life as a series of lessons, you're looking at it through a positive lens. You're giving yourself a positive mindset.

I like to compare goals to the blast range on a mortar. Every mortar has a kill zone depending on the calibre. When you're dropping mortars on an enemy vehicle or a group of combatants, you don't need to score a direct hit. You only need to ensure that the mortar splashes down close enough to the target to do some damage. The resulting shrapnel will take care of anyone in proximity to the blast. You'll still accomplish your mission.

Build flexibility into your goals. Don't make them rigid. If your goals are immoveable and you fall short of them for whatever reason, you're going to turn your victories into defeats.

'If you would be a reader, read; if a writer, write. But if you do not read for a month, but do something else, you'll see the consequences. So after sitting still for ten days, get up and attempt to take a long walk, and you will find how your legs are weakened. Upon the whole, then, whatever you would make habitual, practise it; and if you would not make a thing habitual, do not practise it, but habituate yourself to something else.'

Epictetus, Discourses, Book II, 18.1–4

LESSON 34

DON'T RELY ON OUTSIDE FORCES

From the moment you join the military, you're made to understand that you have a reputation to uphold: the reputation of the British soldier.

The idea that we are the best fighting force in the world is repeatedly drilled into us in training. We're not the biggest army, by far, but we're better than anyone else because of our exceptional discipline. That's why our standards are so high – and why we maintain those standards. Because we're defending our reputation. A reputation that has been forged over the centuries and throughout dramatically varied campaigns. We're the guys who get the job done. And we always deliver.

That's why Selection is the hardest process of its kind anywhere in the world. It pushes you to your physical and psychological extremes. Anyone who can't meet those standards gets culled.

Upholding those standards also means being courageous enough to back up your actions on the ground, not relying on outside forces to come to your rescue. Which is where self-reliance kicks in.

Self-reliance comes from having standards you refuse to compromise on, and hold yourself to, consistently.

The way I saw it, I had voluntarily signed up for hazardous service. No one had forced me to sign up. I was prepared to put myself in dangerous situations. Therefore I could only rely on myself and my muckers to get out of it. No one else is coming to the rescue.

That attitude has always stayed with me. Whatever I'm committing to, whether it's a mountaineering challenge or another adventure, I've always gone in knowing that if I end up in trouble, I'll have to get out of it myself.

When you start to think you can rely on outside help, you're giving yourself false options. Because if the mission goes south, help might never come. Or it might come too late. Telling yourself that if it goes wrong, you'll be alright because someone will pull you out of the fire – that's a huge no-no in our profession. We go in thinking that it's down to us to sort out any problems on the ground. 'We volunteered for this. It's up to us to get out of trouble.'

Elite teams are often their only sources of help. But this doesn't faze them. Because they have the right mindset. They're perfectly comfortable with the situation they find themselves in, even happy with it. Because they believe in themselves and each other.

Outside forces won't save or protect you. Don't wait for someone to come in and rescue you because it might never happen.

The only person who can save you is yourself.

- Don't be afraid of failure. Embrace it. Make it work for you.

- Remember that the hardest lessons in life are the most rewarding. When you find yourself in difficulty, don't give in to despair. Instead, have that rational conversation with yourself. Understand your feelings – where they've come from and why you're experiencing them. Focus your energies on assessing the situation and coming up with strategies to cope and overcome the crisis.

- Have the courage to be honest with yourself. Remind yourself that only good things can come from self-honesty. The more you practise it, the more you'll be open and transparent with other people.

- Never switch off during a task. The consequences could be disastrous.

- When you find yourself in a catastrophic situation, remember that you are always part of a team. You don't have to face your problems alone. Attack them together, with your friends or colleagues or family, and you'll find a way to get through.

- If you happen to find yourself in the Void, get out of it by committing to an action or a goal. Whatever you do, don't give up. Don't accept life in the Void.

- Other people and situations will help to shape you over time, but don't let those things *define* you. Be your own blacksmith. Sharpen your blade in a way that works for you. Seize control of your destiny.

- Understand that you don't need to be perfect. When attacking a goal, you only need to be in the general vicinity of excellence. Just because you didn't hit the bullseye doesn't make you a failure.

- Don't rely on others to come to your rescue. Practise self-reliance and mental resilience. Remember that the only person who can save you is yourself.

PART FIVE

STRATEGIES

LESSON 35

FOCUS ON THE THINGS YOU CAN CONTROL

Panic is infectious.

In the military, you can find yourself in a situation where there are a million things happening at any one time and it's easy to become distracted and overwhelmed. At those moments, it's absolutely vital to focus on yourself. One of the most effective strategies for retaining that control is to remind yourself that most of the things you're worried about are outside your control.

I've been in situations when soldiers have failed to apply this mindset. Panic can affect even the best warriors. In those situations, it's vital to remind each other that panicking isn't going to get you out of trouble. Instead, you have to accept that the situation is outside of your control, calm down and do what needs to be done – and you have to do this fast, because panic is highly infectious. Left unchecked, it will quickly spread, creating a frenzy among the rest of the group. That's when things can go seriously wrong.

Widespread panic achieves absolutely nothing except

allowing the enemy to think they have got the edge over you and your mates.

As a soldier you are going to sometimes find yourself in extremely hazardous or life-threatening situations that are *entirely outside of your control.* That can be frightening for some people. Knowing that nothing you can do will make the slightest difference to your chances of survival.

When you find yourself in that type of situation, it's important to remember that the only thing you can control is your own reaction. Whether you decide to let the external threat influence your behaviour or actions in a negative way. Whether you choose to stay calm, or surrender to the emotions.

How you respond to a threat or an issue, is not just a matter of personal reaction. It will also have a powerful influence on your teammates. If you're anxious, you're going to transmit that to emotion to your muckers. But if you stay composed and think rationally, they're going to follow your lead.

LEARNING TO RECOGNISE THE DIFFERENCE BETWEEN WHAT IS INSIDE AND OUTSIDE YOUR CONTROL IS KEY TO MASTERING YOUR RESPONSE TO SITUATIONS.

In today's world, 'anxiety', 'stress' and 'pressure' are classed as dirty words. It's common to hear someone say, 'I'm anxious,' or 'I'm feeling really stressed right now,' but those are hollow statements unless you're prepared to break them down, to dig into the root causes of *why* you're feeling that way. And key to that is understanding that there can be positive anxiety, just as there's such a thing as positive stress and positive pressure.

Learning to recognise the difference between what is inside and outside your control is key to mastering your response to situations.

Soldiers intrinsically understand this.

If I'm stressed out and feeling the pressure because I'm in charge of a mission that might – if successful – save hundreds of lives, then that is a positive type of stress. Similarly, if your company is given a project that could be a game-changer for your business if you pull it off.

Whenever you're gripped by these feelings, ask yourself, 'Is the purpose I'm aiming towards positive? Is there a big reward potentially waiting for me if I perform to the best of my abilities?' If the answer is 'Yes,' then classify it as a positive stress.

I sometimes find it helpful to flip it round. Try to imagine that you're in charge of a major mission on the ground, or you're negotiating a deal that could send your company into the financial stratosphere. You *should* feel the pressure in that situation! There's a huge opportunity to do something positive. You'd better hope the pressure is on. If you're not feeling stressed, then you're not going to deliver.

The benefits of how much stress you're feeling, or how

much pressure is on you, is directly related to the positive goal or outcome you are progressing towards.

In all those cases, the source of your pressure or anxiety is something that you can *control*. That is what makes it positive. You can influence the result of the business negotiations or use the skills at your disposal to effect a successful outcome to the mission.

If you're anxious about things outside of your control, however, that is negative anxiety.

Negative anxiety is wasted energy. Effort expended for no reward. There's nothing you can do to flip that worry into a positive outcome. Being anxious won't make the situation better. The same goes for stress.

Let's say you're stressed because you've got a massive credit card bill, or you can't afford to pay off your overdraft. If you've got no money, then it's out of your control. In the short-term you can't do anything to change your circumstances. So it's pointless to fret over it. You're better off focusing your efforts elsewhere.

Positive anxiety or stress is like a boxer preparing to enter the ring to contest the world heavyweight championship. It fuels you; it's good that you're feeling that, because you're aware of what's at stake, you're switched on and motivated, and you're more likely to succeed. Whereas negative feelings are self-induced. They're a reaction to external things beyond your control, but your mind wants to try and control them anyway, so it responds by obsessively worrying over them. But that won't make things any better because you can't influence the outcome.

Your overdraft isn't going to get any smaller just because

you're lying awake at night thinking about it. All you're doing is digging yourself into an even bigger hole.

Whenever you're confronted with these feelings, learn to distinguish between the positive and the negative. Ask yourself whether this is something you can take charge of within yourself, or whether this is an external event beyond your control. If the stress or anxiety is negative, stop worrying about it. Why be anxious about something beyond your control?

When people don't make that distinction, they give in to the anxiety, or pressure. They enter a doom loop. They become anxious because they can't do anything about it. But they can't do anything about it, which feeds the anxiety. That negative feeling swells, until it's unmanageable. Then they suffer a breakdown.

What they should be doing in that situation is looking at that specific feeling and asking themselves whether they can put it in the positive spectrum. 'Is it inside my control?' If it is, then you've removed a negative worry and flipped it into a positive. You can then focus on dealing with it and effecting a positive outcome.

Everything in life is either controllable or uncontrollable.

When you learn how to break things down like that, it becomes a very simple process, because it empowers you. It leads you away from the minefield of victimhood.

The victimhood mindset is a cop-out. It doesn't ask whether something is in your control. It encourages you to surrender responsibility, to raise the white flag and say, 'It's not my fault.' Victimhood feeds into a sense of entitlement, which is just as hazardous to achieving success in life. People fall into the trap of thinking, 'I am a victim, therefore I am entitled to X. I am owed this thing I really want.'

The harsh truth is we are entitled to absolutely nothing in life. We owe the world nothing; the world owes us nothing in return. Everything must be earned, nothing can be taken for granted.

When you embrace that thought process, your mindset will start to change. You'll look at something you want and instead of wondering why no one has given it to you, or moaning about how you can't achieve it because of something external, you'll think more positively. 'Right, if I want to get this reward, I'm going to have to go out and really graft for it.'

Along the way, you're going to encounter failure, anxiety, stress, pressure, pain, sacrifice. All of those things will follow. But if you persist with it, once you punch through the wall, you're going to reach the amazing realms of capability, discipline, motivation, self-belief.

Believe it or not, these things all exist on the other side of the wall of so-called negativity. I say 'so-called' because the stuff that's usually labelled negative is actually positive. It's positive because it helps you get to that positive outcome or result.

When you're in a situation outside your control, don't let the panic win. Stay calm. Focus your energies instead on influencing those things within your domain.

'To be near the goal while the enemy is still far from it, to wait at ease while the enemy is toiling and struggling, to be well-fed while the enemy is famished – this is the art of husbanding one's strength.'

Sun Tzu, The Art of War, Chapter 7.31

LESSON 36

MAKE FEAR WORK FOR YOU

Fear is the number one hurdle that stops us from achieving our goals in life. It's there in all of us. Even the bravest soldier knows fear. It doesn't matter how tough you might be, how well trained you are or how many missions you've completed – you can never become fearless. That fear is always going to be present. Anyone who tells you otherwise is lying through their teeth.

What you *can* do is face down fear. Look it in the eye. Break it down. Study it. When you do that, you'll start to see that fear is your body priming itself to step into the unknown. That's what the sensation of fear is: not knowing whether you're going to be good enough to succeed or fail at a given task, whether the outcome is going to be positive, or what people are going to think or say if you don't achieve that ambition. The unknown is a chasm, and fear is you standing on the cliff-edge looking down below.

When you learn to face down fear, it won't paralyse you; instead you'll start to feel alive.

Fear *excites* me. When I feel fear, it's like my body is telling me, 'Get ready! Get ready!' Stepping into the unknown means you're going to learn something, no matter what. Whether you make it to your destination is basically irrelevant. You're entering a new space, a *learning space*. That can only be a positive thing. And when you look at the unknown in a positive light, instead of being afraid, you're going to grow from it, and therefore become a better version of yourself.

WHEN YOU LEARN TO FACE DOWN FEAR, IT WON'T PARALYSE YOU; INSTEAD YOU'LL START TO FEEL ALIVE.

Fear, like all emotions, is triggered by your response to certain situations or individuals. If someone insults you verbally, for example, you can't help how you feel in the moment, no matter how much you try to block it out or tell yourself, 'I don't care what this person says, I won't let it affect me.' The same thing is true with fear. You can't help feeling it – there is no 'Off' switch for fear in your physiological make-up.

Fear can't be conquered, it can't be banished from your life. It is always going to be there in one form or another. But it can be harnessed, and you achieve that by repeatedly exposing yourself to it. When you expose yourself to fear, after a while you'll be able to understand exactly how you are going to feel in a particular situation. And you'll learn how to make that fear work *for* you instead of working *against* you.

This is an ongoing process throughout your life. There is no fast-track when it comes to learning how to harness fear. You can only get to that point by repeatedly exposing yourself to it.

When you find yourself in a dangerous or stressful situation for the first time, adrenaline is going to get you over the line. The next time you find yourself in the same position, you'll have a better idea of what to expect. You'll know how your body is going to react. It becomes that little bit easier to get through. So then you do it again, and again. Gradually, the layers will come off that fear. The more you expose yourself to that situation, the more layers you'll peel off – and the closer you'll get to understanding that emotion. But also – more importantly – you'll learn how to make that emotion *work for you.*

On the battlefield, once you've faced the same hazardous situation many times, you'll go beyond the fear. You'll punch through it. Instead of relying on adrenaline to get you through, you begin to feel a sense of what I can only describe as euphoria. Life becomes drained of complications. Everything is reduced to its purest state. Life and death. Kill or be killed. In that situation there are no grey areas, no uncertainties. Either you're going to survive the mission, or you won't.

Instead of surrendering to fear, through repeated exposure you'll flip that emotion into something that enables you to take charge of the situation.

This is what happens when you harness fear. You reach a point where you are aware of your body preparing itself for the challenge of entering the unknown space. This is equally true in situations where it's not about life or death. In fact, you should be even more excited about fear then, because even if you don't succeed, you'll still be alive. You'll have learned something from the experience. You'll have a valuable tool to take away, put in your toolbox and utilise to your advantage in the future. Then you can re-attack the situation and take another layer off. Keep going and going until you reach the nut. Or you might reach a point where you realise that the path you're currently on won't get you to your goal. In which case, stop and find another way to achieve what you've set out to do. Take another route and try that approach instead.

When you commit to fear, you're always going to take something out of that commitment phase. Because you're committing to *yourself*.

When you commit to yourself, you will realise what you're truly capable of. And when you realise what you're capable of, self-belief will kick in at the back end of that process. Self-belief comes from knowing yourself – and you can only know yourself by learning how to control your emotions and get them to work for you. When you can do that, it's like having a superpower, because whatever situation you find yourself in, you're going to be able to control your emotional response rather than letting it control you. There's not much that will faze you in life.

Let's say you have a fear of heights. Imagine we're standing on top of a cliff, and I tell you to walk to the edge, as close as you can. On the first attempt you might get ten metres from the cliff-edge before you move away from it. Now, the easy thing to do is to look at that movement in a negative light and say, 'I failed. I didn't achieve what I wanted to do.' But you're missing all the steps that you've taken to get closer to the edge of that cliff – all the layers you've taken off that fear. All the tiny percentages that you've chipped away from it during that first attempt.

A negative mindset will never help you harness fear. Instead of telling yourself that you've failed, ask yourself, 'Is that the closest I've ever been to the edge of the cliff?' Or look at it another way: if I asked you to walk ten metres from the cliff-edge again, would you know exactly how you're going to feel? The answer would be, 'Yes.' So now you can harness that, use that awareness of self to try again. This time, once you're ten metres from the edge, you can take another two or three steps forward, reminding yourself to live in the moment, not to get carried away with the destination. You're in a new space, learning from it and growing from it.

Even if it takes you a few hundred attempts to get to the point where you can harness your fear so effectively that you can stand on the cliff-edge, it doesn't matter. It's the process that matters – not the end point.

Nothing in life ever goes from zero to a hundred per cent. You need to go from zero to one, or even zero to zero-point-one. You have to commit to the work. Expose yourself to the fear. Repeat the process. And you have to be prepared to do this consistently, throughout your life, in order to keep a hold on that fear, to turn it into something approaching muscle memory. Otherwise there's a chance it might grow back.

Expose yourself to fear. Confront it *repeatedly*. Each time you do, you'll gain a bit more control of it, and you'll therefore develop a sense of achievement and reward. No one else can give you this, though. This is something that you can only gift yourself through repeated commitment to that exposure.

Take the fear off, layer by layer. Learn how to harness that particular feeling in that moment. Accumulate those exposures, learn from them, and use them to your advantage – to help you get to where you need to be in your life.

MASTERING FEAR IN THE ROMAN ARMY

The scene was Gaul, during Julius Caesar's conquest in the winter of 54–53 BC. A tribe called the Eburones had rebelled against the Romans. Their warriors, along with their allies, had slaughtered a load of Roman soldiers after they had been tricked into leaving their heavily defended stronghold.

A smaller force of Romans was garrisoned in the territory of another tribe. Caesar had given their commanding officer strict orders not to leave the camp under any circumstances. But after seven days, with no word on when Caesar might return, the commander decided to send out a foraging party. He reckoned that the enemy would be too scattered and weak to attempt a large-scale attack on the camp while the soldiers were away.

Things quickly went south. While the foragers were out gathering corn, the men left behind at the camp came under attack. The Romans were taken by surprise and barely managed to hold off the initial assault. As the enemy swarmed round all sides of the camp, looking for a suitable breaching point, panic and confusion spread through the defenders. These men had heard of the massacre at Aduatuca. Now they feared they were going to suffer the same fate.

At this point a senior army officer called Publius Baculus stepped up. Baculus had been forced to stay behind at the camp on the grounds of ill-health. He hadn't eaten for several days, so he was hardly in prime fighting condition, but that didn't stop him from taking matters into his own hands. He armed himself and, with a handful of other officers, managed to hold off the enemy warriors attempting to breach the main gate.

This took serious courage. Even though he was wounded multiple times during the fighting, Baculus held his ground until he was too weak to continue; the others just about managed to drag his unconscious body away. Meanwhile the rest of the garrison, inspired by Baculus's example, regained their confidence and ran over to take up their defensive positions.

That wasn't the end of the crisis. As the foraging party made its way back from the corn fields, they came under heavy attack. The Roman soldiers were mostly young recruits with no fighting experience, and they became paralysed with indecision and fear. Some of them argued they should make a stand on top of the nearest hill, but a few veterans knew this was a stupid plan. The Romans were hugely outnumbered and they wouldn't have a chance of defending themselves. Instead the veterans decided to cut their way through the enemy and make for the camp; most of them reached their muckers safely. The men left behind on the hill realised that they had screwed up. They were cut down on lower ground while attempting to fight their way back to the camp. A few lucky guys managed to get through, but the rest were surrounded and killed.

Faced with the prospect of assaulting a well-defended camp, the enemy gave up and legged it back across the Rhine.

When people talk about the strengths of the Roman army they tend to focus on its tactics, organisation and weaponry, but what's often overlooked is the emotional intelligence and resilience of its soldiers. Through relentless exposure to fear in battle and training, these men learned how to control their emotions. How to control fear.

So when the camp came under attack, Baculus didn't panic. Unlike some of his fellow soldiers, fear didn't immobilise him, or cause him to run around like a headless chicken. He didn't let his emotions win. As an experienced officer, Baculus would have exposed himself to fear lots of times in previous campaigns. At the moment of crisis, he was able to control his emotions. He made fear work *for* him, not *against* him. Baculus was able to take charge of the situation, and in doing so he saved the Roman camp, and his mates, from total disaster.

'I must die, and must I die groaning too? I must
be fettered; must I be lamenting too? I must
be exiled; and what hinders me, then, but that
I may go smiling, and cheerful, and serene?'

Epictetus, Discourses, Book I, 1.21

LESSON 37
SHUT OUT NEGATIVITY

Evil exists in the world. Injustice exists. Life can be unfair. Things can – and do – go wrong.

It's easy to get swept up in the idea that the world is a chaotic place, full of spiteful and wicked people; that nothing works, no one is to be trusted. That's the power of the negative narrative. It thrives on feeding you a relentless diet of chaos and drama. It encourages you to look at the world through a wholly negative lens. And it can be hard to get your shield out and bat that stuff away when you're constantly inundated with it.

Every time you switch on the TV, or scroll through the news on your phone, you're subjected to an assault of negativity. The negative mindset, whether you're aware of it or not, is waging a never-ending campaign against your brain, forcing it down your throat. This mentality has conditioned us: it's indoctrinated us into accepting negativity as the normal way of looking at things.

So how do you survive? How do you overcome the negativity mindset that pervades every nook and cranny of our society?

By *shrinking negativity* in your life.

You can't eliminate negativity completely. It has its place in each of us, just like every other part of our minds and bodies. But a negative-dominant attitude will stop you from realising your goals. To live with negativity, you need to reduce it. Like dialling down the volume on your headphones, so the negative part of your mindset is only five or ten per cent, instead of ninety-five per cent of what you hear.

Being point man taught me the importance of this approach. You need to have total confidence and trust in yourself, and you cannot do that if you're carrying around an ounce of negativity. If you're standing outside a door and thinking, 'What if this goes wrong? What if I get shot?', you'll never push through.

I used to play a risk assessment game with myself on missions. I might be outside a room, bullets flying around us, and I'd ask myself, 'What are the chances of the enemy shooting me in the head and killing me outright?' Very slim, probably one per cent, because I'll be moving through that door in a certain way. Besides, I'm the hunter in this situation. The enemy is the prey. And I know how the mind works when you find yourself being hunted.

Then I'd think, 'What are the chances I'll get shot in the chest?' Higher, certainly, because the central mass is the biggest target to aim for. But it's still no more than a fifty-fifty chance. Even if the other guy does get his shot away first, either I'm going to drop him, or my pals behind me will do it for me.

When you frame it like that, the odds are actually looking really good. They're hugely in my favour in that situation. I'm likely to get a favourable outcome by going through that door.

Of course, there's a small chance it'll go wrong. I might go through that door and take a round to the head. But if that happens, I won't know about it. I'm far more likely to clear the room, deal with any threats inside. In which case I'm one step closer to completing the mission. Or I might get shot and survive my injuries. But in that case, I'm still winning because I'm still alive, I'm still breathing. Either way, the potential rewards of going through that door are absolutely huge, and the downsides are miniscule. I'm in a very good position.

This is also applicable to civilian life. It's easy to outsize the risks of doing something and shrink the upside by focusing on that tiny percentage of something going wrong. We tend to let that iota of negative possibility cloud our perception of the whole, especially when we're faced with an important project or mission.

Everything positive has a negative side. Right can't exist without wrong. Good wouldn't exist without evil. That arrogant streak might save you or your mates one day. When you view things through a negative prism, you're not allowing yourself to see the positive flip side.

A few years ago, I was trimming one of the oak trees in our back garden. This tree was really tall, so I'd used my telescopic ladder to get up to the higher branches.

So there I was, sitting on a big old branch on this oak tree, roughly four metres off the ground. Not a great height, not enough to cause serious injury if you fell off the branch. But still high enough that you'd do yourself a little bit of damage.

As I was sitting there, my daughter came out of the house and approached the ladder. She started climbing the steps. She got to a height of about two metres, then stopped.

'What's wrong?' I asked. 'Come up here and sit with Dad.'

'But I'm *high*, Daddy,' my daughter said. 'What if I fall off?'

'What if you don't?' I replied.

That's how I wanted my daughter to view the situation. There's Daddy, sitting up on the branch in the tree. If you don't fall off, then you get to sit up there, and you'll have successfully climbed that ladder. It's an achievement. And it worked: my daughter climbed the rest of the way up the ladder. Joined me on the oak-tree branch. She succeeded because I'd given her a positive approach to the problem in front of her. Whereas people tend to reach straight away for the negative. 'What if X happens? What if I can't do this? What if I'm not physically capable, or I can't harness my emotions?'

Ask yourself: How do you see the world? Do you see it through a positive lens? If not, then your mind is working against you, and you're going to be in a constant battle with yourself. The positives are going to be right in front of you, but you won't notice them, because in your mind you'll have shrunk them down to the size of atoms. Opportunities will pass you by.

If you look at things positively, you're still going to see the negatives, but you'll learn to avoid them. They won't dominate your outlook.

Don't focus on the negative. Have the courage to turn down the volume on your doubts and go through that door. Stop asking yourself, 'What if it goes wrong?' Ask yourself instead, 'What happens if it goes *right*?'

PELOPIDAS AND EPAMINONDAS: MASTERS OF THE MILITARY MINDSET

For many years, the people of Thebes had been under the thumb of the Spartans. But after a coup d'état against the Spartan regime in late 379 BC, a pair of leading Thebans, Pelopidas and Epaminondas, set about transforming the fortunes of the downtrodden city-state.

Key to their success was changing the mindset of young Thebans, helping them to get rid of their inferiority complex towards the Spartans.

Before the coup, Epaminondas used to encourage Theban youths to wrestle against Spartans in the gymnastic schools. Whenever one of the Thebans won a bout, instead of congratulating him, Epaminondas would tear into the victor, telling him to hang his head in shame. Only a coward, Epaminondas said, would allow himself to remain a slave of the Spartans, when it was obvious that they were much physically stronger than their opponents.

Over the next few years, the Spartans sent troops against the Thebans in an attempt to crush them. The Thebans only committed their men to small-scale skirmishes, withdrawing before the enemy could reorganise and re-attack. This gave the Thebans a taste of victory, demonstrating to the lads that they could hold their own against the Spartans.

Matters came to a head at the Battle of Tegyra in 375 BC. Pelopidas's men were faced by a much larger force of Spartans. The Thebans had never beaten the Spartans in a major engagement; the Spartans had never lost to an enemy of the same or smaller size in open battle.

When one of the Thebans caught sight of the advancing Spartan army, he ran over to Pelopidas, shouting anxiously, 'We have fallen into our enemy's hands!'

'Why not the enemy into our hands?' Pelopidas replied.

It would have been all too easy for Pelopidas to panic in that situation. To look at the sheer size of the enemy in front of him, give in to the negative mindset and tell himself, 'Shit, we're going to lose.' But he didn't. He refused to shrink down the positives in his mind. He stayed mentally strong. Pelopidas trusted in his preparations and the abilities of his soldiers. His own skills as a commander. And he was proved right: the Thebans won the day.

'Order not your life as though you had ten thousand years to live. Fate hangs over you. While you live, while yet you may, be good.'

Marcus Aurelius, Meditations, Book 4.17

LESSON 38

TAKE THE HARDEST PATH

When it comes to any military operation the hardest path is almost always the best and most effective option – because it's the one the enemy will least expect you to take.

Elite forces are elite because they've been trained to operate in every kind of environment on the planet. They're conditioned to accomplish what others might consider to be impossible. So they're not afraid to take the hardest path. Throughout history, great battlefield commanders and warriors have asked themselves, 'What's the most difficult route to the enemy stronghold? Where do the enemy think it's impossible for us to attack from? Right, that's the path we're taking.'

Enemies will usually organise their defences according to the likelihood of an assault. If X and Y are the easiest approaches, they'll concentrate their defensive positions at those points. Whereas they might leave Z poorly defended because they won't believe it's possible for anyone to attack from that direction. Therefore, if we take that path, even though it's going to be really hard work, we're going to surprise the enemy. We'll gain a crucial advantage. Taking the hard way is a question of mastering your headspace. Once you condition your mind to accept that the hardest way is the best, it becomes the *only way*. It becomes the norm.

The psychological advantage of taking the impossible path is huge. When you make it through to the other side, you'll get a powerful reward. Suddenly you'll realise, 'Wow, we've done that.'

Our mindset is what makes us the best warfighters in the world. We're thinking soldiers. We're prepared to take the less obvious route to mission success. And we're willing to go places no one else would dare to go.

Our mindset is unique. 'Put your house on your back.' That's our bread and butter. It's a way of thinking that is completely detached from any other line of work. We're operating at a different level from the rest of society. Even professional athletes don't push themselves the way we do.

TAKING THE HARD WAY IS A QUESTION OF MASTERING YOUR HEADSPACE. ONCE YOU CONDITION YOUR MIND TO ACCEPT THAT THE HARDEST WAY IS THE BEST, IT BECOMES THE *ONLY WAY.* IT BECOMES THE NORM.

The hardest path is always the most rewarding. If you're tackling a familiar challenge at work, avoiding the path of least resistance and attempting it from another direction is an excellent way of pushing yourself and staying sharp. In those situations, tell yourself that the hard way is the only path open to you.

Then put your house on your back and get moving.

GENGHIS KHAN AND THE MONGOL ARMY – TAKING THE LEAST EXPECTED PATH

Temüjin, better known to history as Genghis Khan, was born some time between 1155 and 1167, the son of a minor chieftain. He had a rough childhood – his father was murdered while Temüjin was still a boy, and for several years his family struggled to survive. Before long, however, the young Temüjin had built up a loyal following. He struck key alliances and gradually expanded his power base, bringing neighbouring clans under his control. By 1206 he had succeeded in uniting all the tribes of Mongolia.

The Mongols were born to fight. Life on the steppes of central Asia was a constant struggle; from a young age they learned to live with pain, hunger and deprivation. In that environment, only the strongest survived. Mongol kids were taught to ride early in childhood and spent much of their time hunting for game, becoming skilled in the use of the composite bow, hunting traps and the lasso. As nomads, they lived on horseback and roamed across large swathes of territory, so they were used to travelling huge distances, and they knew the land inside out. In extreme circumstances, where no other nourishment was available, a Mongol could survive by opening the neck vein on his horse and drinking the blood.

The Mongols had a well-worked method of waging war. Their lightly armed archers would first soften up the enemy ranks with a barrage of missile fire, spreading chaos and panic. Once the generals judged that the moment was right, they would send in the heavy cavalry to cut them to shreds. If for some reason that didn't work – if the enemy maintained its formation despite the onslaught of arrows and stones – the Mongols would feign flight, drawing the enemy on before turning to charge them.

The Mongols were also brilliant problem-solvers. Each time they ran into a new or unforeseen obstacle, they learned from their mistake, regrouped and found a solution.

When Genghis Khan began his campaign for world conquest, the nomadic Mongols had absolutely no knowledge of siege warfare. Soon, however, they had mastered the use of catapults and incendiaries, and how to mine under the walls of fortified cities. They played psychological tricks on the enemy, mounting straw figures on the backs of their spare horses to give the impression that their army was much bigger than it actually was. Sometimes they would create a smokescreen by burning reeds in order to hide their movements. The Mongols even became skilled in amphibious operations in later years and launched multiple invasions of feudal Japan.

On campaign, the Mongols would take the less obvious path, relying on their advantages in speed, mobility and range to surprise the enemy. This was brilliantly demonstrated during Genghis Khan's invasion of the Khwarazmian Empire in 1219. The Shah expected the Mongols to advance on his lands from the direction of a mountain pass known as the Dzungarian Gate. That was the obvious route of attack. Instead the Mongols invaded from multiple directions. One force advanced from the direction of the north-east. A smaller force under General Jebei crossed the Tian Shan mountains in the depths of winter, enduring freezing cold temperatures, terrible hunger and snowstorms. Meanwhile the main Mongol column under Genghis himself trekked more than four hundred kilometres across the searing Kyzylkum desert, before hooking round to attack from the west, marching on the Khwarazm capital at Samarkand (now in modern-day Uzbekistan).

Realising that he was in danger of being completely encircled, the Shah panicked and fled the country. He later died on an island in the Caspian Sea. By 1221 the war was won.

'Because the Romans did in these instances what all prudent princes ought to do, who have to regard not only present troubles, but also future ones, for which they must prepare with every energy, because, when foreseen, it is easy to remedy them; but if you wait until they approach, the medicine is no longer in time because the malady has become incurable . . .

Therefore, the Romans, foreseeing troubles, dealt with them at once, and, even to avoid a war, would not let them come to a head, for they knew that war is not to be avoided, but is only to be put off to the advantage of others.'

Machiavelli, The Prince, Chapter III

LESSON 39
NEGOTIATE OBSTACLES

There's an old saying in the military: 'Always find a way over, through, under or round an obstacle.'

On the battlefield, everything is merely an obstacle to be overcome. Whatever might be blocking our path, whether it's a river crossing or a mountain, we're not going to let it get in the way of completing the mission.

You will face obstacles in your life. The road to success isn't easy and there will be times where you're being blocked by something outside of your control. Whether you're switching careers, trying to lose weight, starting a business. Whatever. There will be setbacks. There will be roadblocks. What's important is how you face these moments, and how you overcome them.

Obstacles are a challenge we can either accept or decline. You can't ignore them. They might be the only thing stopping you from taking that next step. Don't deviate from your goal. Keep the momentum and keep moving forward. These moments can present opportunities for you, but you won't know until you've tackled the problem head on.

Take your time to size up an obstacle in your path. Gather your information. Approach it strategically. Find out the best way to negotiate it, whether that's up, over, under or around. When you study an obstacle, you're going to stand a much better chance of overcoming or defeating it. It's how you respond to challenges and obstacles in your way that will define who you are.

ALEXANDER THE GREAT AND THE ROCK OF SOGDIANA

One of history's greatest generals, Alexander the Great, brilliantly demonstrated the power of this mindset.

In 327 BC, during his campaign to conquer the Achaemenid Empire, a nomadic and warlike people called the Sogdians had taken refuge in their mountain fortress.

The defenders were safe in their fortress – or at least that's what they thought. Everyone assumed their fortress, the Sogdian Rock, was impossible to capture. The sides were very steep, and a recent spell of heavy snowfall made the approach even more perilous. The rebels were well stocked, with enough provisions and water to withstand a long siege. When Alexander called on the rebels to surrender, they were so confident of their position that they boasted that the Macedonian soldiers would need wings if they were going to capture it.

Saying that to Alexander was like waving a red rag at a bull. Alexander was a figure of almost superhuman self-belief. He didn't believe in 'can't' or 'won't' or 'shouldn't'. This was a man who marched his army across extreme desert for two months, simply because he wanted to succeed where others had failed.

Alexander set to work. He assembled a force of three hundred men with some rock-climbing experience. In the evening, they crept towards the steepest side of the Rock, following the oldest rule in warfare: always hit the enemy where they least expect it. Alexander knew that this would be the least well-defended approach, precisely because it was the hardest one to climb up.

Under cover of darkness, the men began their ascent, using iron tent pegs with ropes attached as makeshift ice picks. Thirty men plunged to their deaths, but the rest managed to reach the top of the mountain. At dawn they waved a set of flags, giving the pre-arranged signal to Alexander that they had taken possession of the summit. When the Sogdians were alerted to the soldiers on the crest, panic set in and they quickly surrendered, thinking they were facing a much larger force.

When you find yourself confronted by your own Rock, when your way is blocked by a seemingly insurmountable obstacle, remember: there is always a way up, or around, or through. No hurdle in your life cannot be navigated if you are prepared to apply yourself fully to the challenge.

BE FORWARD THINKING

When things go wrong, don't panic. Don't reach for the easiest solution or do something purely because it's the honourable or morally right thing to do. Think about it.

Think ahead.

Take the idea of leaving no man behind. It sounds heroic in principle. But when you think it through, it's not always the best idea.

If we've been heavily compromised at the extraction point, for example, two of my mates have been taken out and we're about to be overrun, am I going to run for the extraction vehicle? Damn right I will. If I can take you with me then I will, but if I can't, what's the point of the rest of us going down guns blazing? Two dead men is a tragedy; four dead men on the ground is a PR victory for the enemy. They can drag our bodies through the village, pose with us in front of the cameras, big grins on their faces. By fighting to the death all we've accomplished is to give the bad guys the upper hand.

But if I *can* get off the ground, here's what is going to happen. I can take the important intelligence – everything I've seen and heard – back with me. Grab some bods and talk them through the intel. What weapons the enemy have got, how many buildings are in the area, whether there are any booby traps or IEDs on-site. Then we can go back in, repatriate the bodies, wipe out the rest of the enemy combatants and complete the mission.

CULTIVATE THE MINDSET OF THE THINKING SOLDIER.

'Leave no man behind,' isn't the mindset of the thinking soldier. By all means try to get your pals out of trouble. But if you're seriously compromised, then it's better to get back, so you can tell your side of the story. That's your choice: do you want a one-sided story, or two sides?

Cultivate the mindset of the thinking soldier. When you're faced with a personal or professional crisis, don't reach for the pre-cut solution. Be forward thinking. Ask yourself what you can change and use it to the advantage of yourself or your organisation. Then act on it.

THEMISTOCLES AND
THE WOODEN WALL

The Athenian noble Themistocles was a true forward thinker. In 490 BC, the Persians had suffered a shock defeat at the Battle of Marathon. Most Athenians believed that was the end of the threat from Persia, but Themistocles knew better. He reckoned that the Persians would return one day to avenge their humiliation. So while everyone else was celebrating victory, he turned his mind to the next war.

Themistocles first persuaded his fellow citizens to divert the profits from a silver mine towards building up the navy. He did this by pretending that the ships would be used for a war against one of their hated neighbours – the Greeks were always squabbling among themselves back then. The assembly agreed to his proposal and the fleet – the so-called 'Wooden Wall' – was built.

This was a big moment for Themistocles. The Athenians traditionally relied on the strength of their infantry to win their wars. There wasn't any great enthusiasm for creating a huge fleet. But Themistocles kept making his case because he understood that a strong navy would help them in the coming clash with the Persians. On top of this, he also persuaded the other states to work together. Only by setting aside their differences and ending the constant infighting, Themistocles knew, would they stand a chance of resisting their common enemy.

In 480 BC, following the defeat of King Leonidas and his Spartans at the Battle of Thermopylae, the Greek fleet put in at the straits of Salamis, a small island situated a few kilometres to the west of Athens.

The city was in a state of panic. The Persian land army was closing in, and there was a mad rush to evacuate before the enemy arrived at the gates. Meanwhile, the crews on the Greek ships readied themselves for battle.

While Athens burned, there was a furious debate among the naval commanders about what to do next. Some felt they should sail out of Salamis and make for the coast at the Isthmus of Corinth, which was still under Greek control. The commanders worried that if they stayed where they were and lost, they would have nowhere to go.

Themistocles, in overall command of the navy, realised that leaving Salamis would be a tactical error. They were in a good defensive position, and he knew they could beat the Persians at sea, because he'd seen them fight at an earlier engagement. Although they hadn't won on that occasion, the Greeks had more than held their own against the Persian fleet.

So when Adeimantus, the commander of the Corinthian ships, tried to force the issue, Themistocles stood his ground. He even threatened to sail off with the Athenian vessels unless Adeimantus went along with his plan. Despite this U-turn, however, the Peloponnesians in the fleet were still determined to quit Salamis. Themistocles realised his carefully laid plans were about to collapse.

He therefore took decisive action. Without telling anyone else, he ordered one of his slaves to secretly make his way to the enemy fleet, bearing a message for the Persian king, Xerxes. The slave claimed that Themistocles was actually on the Persian side, that the Greek captains were planning to escape, and therefore Xerxes should attack at once before they could slip away.

Xerxes fell for the trick, partly because the message reinforced his own beliefs about the Greeks and their flimsy alliance. Some of the city-states had already gone over to his side and Xerxes had every reason to think that the Greek fleet might break up as soon as they saw his ships approaching.

On his orders two hundred Persian vessels surrounded the straits, blocking the exits and trapping the Greeks inside. When the Greeks realised they were sealed in, they had no option but to engage the enemy – just as Themistocles had correctly foreseen.

At dawn the next day the Persians made their move. In the narrow confines of the straits the Persian armada was forced to attack in detachments, denying them the advantage of numerical superiority. Although they had a reputation as skilled seamen, the Persians struggled to manoeuvre in the straits and the Greek strategy of rowing at speed towards the enemy and ramming them worked brilliantly. By the evening the Greeks had emerged victorious. Forty thousand men had been killed on the Persian side. The survivors sailed away.

Victory, masterminded by Themistocles, would have far-reaching consequences for the future of the West, laying the groundwork for the Greeks' decisive victories over the Persians the following year.

BE ADAPTABLE

Versatility is one of the most underrated skillsets of any military force. It might not sound as glamorous as being a first-class sniper or assaulting an enemy stronghold, or whatever it might be. But staying fluid is just as crucial to mission success.

Plans are always helpful, of course. But you've got to be able to adapt to events on the ground, because you never know exactly what's going to happen.

Mike Tyson put it best when he said that everyone has a plan until they get punched in the mouth. The plan might go up in smoke as soon as that first round goes off. Someone might get shot or blown up, or the target might make a run for it. Or you might come up against unexpectedly stiff resistance. I could find myself in a firefight with four or five enemy combatants because they've been alerted to our presence. In which case the original plan to clear the buildings in a certain order goes out of the window.

When the shit hits the fan, you need to be able to adapt

to the new situation. Find a way to deal with the unexpected or new threat. And you need to be able to do it in a split-second. That means being able to figure it out as you go. Learning to adapt to events on the ground as they happen in real-time.

For me, that was the most exciting part of the job. Knowing that you're going to need to problem-solve in a fraction of a second – and accepting that you're not always going to get it right.

Going in with that mindset allowed me to recover from my mistakes. I knew I wasn't always going to get it right because I'm only human. When you're making split-second decisions in the heat of a mission, you're never going to be right all the time. But I always tried to solve the problem to the best of my ability. I always felt that I had made the right decision based upon the situation and the information available to me at the time. So even when it turned out that I'd made the wrong choice, I didn't take it personally. The challenge then became how to adapt. How to rectify the problem or mistake so we could salvage the mission.

The priority is always the same. Adapt to the situation in front of you. Don't waste vital seconds beating yourself up when things go wrong. Recover from your setbacks. Reorganise and re-attack the problem from a different direction. Keep going until you find a solution.

Selection is designed for you to fail. This is what makes it such a clever process. During the course, you're repeatedly led to believe that you've failed. To make it through, you need to be mentally resilient and confident enough to convince yourself not to worry. You need to tell yourself that you're still in the game. That you're going to find a solution.

If you can adapt your mind to convince yourself that the setback in front of you is actually a stepping stone to lead you on to the next lesson or the next goal, then you'll have an incredibly powerful weapon in your mental armoury.

As a soldier, being adaptable is massively important if we're going to overcome the hurdles and complete the mission. Sometimes we don't have specific information on a particular target or building – but in those cases we don't rely on assumptions. That's when you need to go back to relying on your training and discipline. Which feeds directly into adaptability, because you have an underlying set of principles that you're able to call upon and utilise depending on the specific situation on the ground.

The Chicago Bulls under Phil Jackson and his assistant Tex Winter mastered the triangular offense. Their rivals had begun to deliberately target Michael Jordan to limit his effectiveness, but by deploying the triangular system, with the players moving in such a way that they were all supporting each other, Jackson made his team unbeatable. The Bulls were able to adapt their game to meet the new challenges they faced, and as a result, they won multiple titles.

Elite military forces operate in the same way. It's a process of constant tactical *adaption and evolution*. It's about finding the best way of completing the mission through a combination of training and trial and error, learning from each other's mistakes – and then tweaking the system to stay one step ahead of the game.

Adaptability isn't just about the physical situation on the ground, though. Far from it. On the modern battleground, adaptability is also about soldiers being versatile internally, *within themselves*, on the emotional level.

In the purest sense of the word, adaptability is emotional. The body will follow where the mind takes it.

To be an effective soldier, I needed to adapt my inner self. I had to be able to recognise when an emotion presented itself naturally, and I had to know when that feeling had been triggered by a thought process – that I might not even be in the situation that was making me feel that way and respond accordingly.

Emotional adapatability is the hallmark of a good soldier. The very best warfighters have the ability to jump from one end of the emotional spectrum to the other, within a few seconds, in the middle of a firefight. They can be pumped up one moment, taking down bad guys, running on adrenaline and doing the business, like a dog with a bloodlust. Then suddenly they'll find themselves in an entirely different situation. It might be discovering a room full of hostages, for example. At which point they have to instantly adapt their mindset. Being able to jump from code red aggression to feeling compassion and empathy – that's what elite soldiering is all about.

That's what I mean by adaptability in the emotional sense of the word. But you can only learn about this by putting yourself out there, by exposing yourself to situations where you need to commit to action and make quick decisions.

Only by analysing your emotions and their accompanying thought processes will you learn about the power of the mind over the body. Once you understand that, you'll be able to recover from setbacks and modify your approach to ensure a better chance of success in whatever you do.

GENERAL GIAP: THE 'RED NAPOLEON'

General Vo Nguyen Giap was a master of battlefield flexibility. In 1954, during the last months of the Indochina War, he masterminded a spectacular victory over the French that brought an end to nearly eight years of bloodshed.

French Union forces had occupied a series of fortified positions around the valley of Dien Bien Phu. The basic plan was to use the base to forward-mount ops against the enemy, patrolling the surrounding area and blocking the enemy's supply lines from Laos.

But Dien Bien Phu also served another purpose. Giap's men were experts at guerrilla warfare. The French knew they didn't stand a chance of defeating him in the jungle. So they decided to use their base to bait the enemy into launching a large-scale assault – exactly the kind of fighting that suited the French, allowing them to use their artillery and air support to smash the enemy. In reality they were making the same mistake the Persians had at Gaugamela, thinking that they could beat the enemy by controlling the conditions of battle.

The French misjudged Giap. When the time came to begin the main assault he considered the scale of the challenge in front of him. His men were facing more than 10,000 soldiers, backed up with air support, tanks and artillery fire and bedded down in several heavily defended positions. He knew that if he went ahead with his plan, there was a chance it might go badly wrong. Even if they did beat the French, their casualties would have been massive. So Giap took the braver path. He looked at the situation and changed his mind. Instead of recklessly throwing forward massed waves of infantry, Giap decided they would besiege the enemy.

His men dug a system of trenches around Dien Bien Phu. Artillery pieces were transported across difficult terrain – something the French didn't think was possible – and positioned around the hills overlooking the basin. Because Giap had no Forward Air Controllers (FACs) he had to improvise by placing his guns in tunnels dug into the forward slopes of hills instead of putting them on reverse, giving them direct line-of-sight to the enemy. From here they could target the airstrips to prevent the French from getting resupply from the air.

In mid-March Giap attacked. The defenders, inspired by the example of Major Marcel 'Bruno' Bigeard, showed incredible determination and courage, killing thousands of attackers, even as their position became increasingly hopeless. Giap then changed his tactics again and concentrated his efforts on encircling the French by digging trenches to bring his troops closer to the remaining strongpoints.

The defenders were low on food, ammunition and medical supplies. The air bridge had been knocked out, so they had to rely on air-drops. Many of these fell off-target and were gobbled up by the enemy.

By early May it was over. The final positions were overrun, and the survivors taken prisoner, apart from a handful of men who managed to flee into the surrounding jungle. The military genius of General Giap had seen a force of guerrilla fighters defeat a professional army.

'A prince, therefore, being compelled knowingly
to adopt the beast, ought to choose the fox
and the lion; because the lion cannot defend
himself against snares and the fox cannot
defend himself against wolves. Therefore,
it is necessary to be a fox to discover the
snares and a lion to terrify the wolves.'

Machiavelli, The Prince, Chapter XVIII

LESSON 42

ORGANISE YOUR CAGE

We all know that the human mind is unfathomably complicated. Your brain is your own personal supercomputer. People
can – and do – build ideas in their heads that they absolutely
believe to be true. These ideas end up destroying them
because they're unable to separate reality from unreality. And
yet despite this, we insist on adding layers of complication on
top of an already complex network – even when it triggers a
psychological fracturing or meltdown.

If you have too many moving parts in your head, you're
going to be distracted and, ultimately, overwhelmed. The key
to avoiding this outcome is to keep things as simple as possible in whatever you're doing. And that means learning to
compartmentalise.

Ideally, you should compartmentalise in everything you do.
Weave it into the fabric of your daily existence. In doing so, you'll
create a simple yet efficient system for managing life's problems.

We all subconsciously compartmentalise to some degree.
But to achieve tangible results in your life, you need to do it

consciously and consistently. Start by asking yourself, 'Is there a crossover between this problem and that problem? Is there a common denominator here?' If there is, then you should lump those problems together. If not, keep them separate and solve them individually.

When people fail to do this in their lives, it's like dumping a load of files on your desktop screen, instead of organising them into different folders. Or writing a book, but not bothering to organise the material into chapters, paragraphs or subheadings. All you're left with is an incoherent mess.

The external reflects the internal. We probably all know someone who's surrounded by mess in their own home. Nine times out of ten, that person won't be able to separate things out in their head or keep them distinct. They'll probably be disorganised in the way they think.

When you're not compartmentalising, it becomes very difficult to concentrate on any one task. You lose the ability to focus. You're too busy thinking about something in your head, rather than looking at the problem right in front of you. Therefore you won't get the best out of yourself. You won't succeed at your mission or gain a better understanding of it.

It can be helpful to visualise compartmentalisation as a cutlery drawer in your kitchen. Everything in that drawer is neatly divided into different sections: knives, forks, spoons and so on. When you think, 'I need the tin opener,' you know exactly which compartment to go to. If everything was just dumped in there, you'd have to waste time looking for the right utensil. It would take you longer to find what you're looking for.

When everything is organised, it's like creating a fast-track system inside your head. You can reach for the thing you need, without having to think about it. Life becomes that one or two per cent less complicated.

As a soldier I always made sure my kit was neatly ordered. If one of my pals asked me for a combination tool, I could tell him where to find it – without even thinking about it. 'Go into my locker, mate. Left-hand side, second drawer to the right. Open that up, you'll see a green wallet. Unzip that and you'll find the tool in there.' Weapon-cleaning kit, ghillie suit, camo-cream: everything was categorised, everything had its place. Although these things all came under the umbrella category of my personal kit, I had sub-divided them into different sections.

I was making life easier for myself.

When you do this externally, organising your physical environment, you'll be able to visualise the system in your head. You'll carry round a facsimile of that ordered cage or room that you can instantly access at any time. But it doesn't work the other way round: you can't see something clearly if you can't visualise it on the outside.

If you invest the time and effort to put this into practice in your daily life, you'll develop the ability to think more clearly and in a more focused way. It could be something as simple as how you order your textbooks in your schoolbag. My system would be to arrange my books by order of lessons, so if maths was my first lesson of the day, that would go at the back of the bag. When I'm done with that book, I'll put it at the front of the bag. At the start of every lesson, I don't have to spend time rooting around in my bag, looking for the right book. I just reach for the one at the back, and I'll know that's the one I need, because I've created a system.

STRUCTURING YOUR MIND IS INCREDIBLY IMPORTANT IN TERMS OF DECISION-MAKING. IT ALL COMES BACK TO BEING PRESENT IN THE MOMENT.

This sounds very simple, but it's these small things that will help make your life easier, and lead to you making better decisions generally.

The great thing about compartmentalising is that once you have a system, you can mix it up, so you gain the benefits of staying sharp. Changing the order will keep you mentally on your toes.

Structuring your mind is incredibly important in terms of decision-making. It all comes back to being present in the moment. If you're distracted, your head's not in the game. Your mind is elsewhere, you won't be fully focused on the task, and you're not going to think it through clearly. That will impact negatively on your ability to make better life choices.

Keeping it simple is an overused term, but when it comes to the mind it's essential. Your mind is already hypercomplicated. If you add layers of complexity on top of that, you're going to overthink. And you'll mess up.

This is also vital when prioritising tasks. You won't be able to judge the importance of something unless you have a fixed structure in your mind, unless your thoughts are organised systematically. And you can only gain that through internal compartmentalisation. One isn't possible without the other. If your thoughts are all over the place, how are you going to know what's important to you? What needs to be done, and what can be put on the backburner?

Suppose you want to improve your fitness. You might decide to train your upper body on day one, your core muscles on day two, and work on your legs on day three. That's your system.

When I'm going down to the sniper range, I'll have a mental checklist of what I need to do before I start putting down rounds. First, I'll get the rounds out and make sure they're up to scratch. Then I'll oil up my mags, head down to the range. Attach my scope. That's my routine. Someone else might start off by checking their sights before they move on to oiling the mags. There's no one set system: everyone will have a different way of organising and structuring things in their head.

Soldiers need to be able to make decisions in a heartbeat. When I'm point man on the team and I'm standing outside a room, and bullets are flying through the door, I don't have ten minutes to reach a decision on what to do next. I've got seconds. Maybe less. You can't risk going into that situation with a disordered mind.

If you're not organised, internally and externally, you're lost.

To be hyperfocused, you need to be able to isolate each task in turn. Focus on the thing in front of you. I like to think of it in visual terms. It's like accessing a folder in my head. I'll double-click on the folder marked, 'Room clearances'. Okay, what's the next step here? How am I going to get this done?

All the information I need is there in front of me. I can reach a decision in milliseconds. Put a green tick or a red cross next to that file or folder, drag it over, put it in the bin. Reach for the next item.

You don't need to visualise things in this particular way. This is just how I do it. No one can tell you what will work for you: you can only find this out through trial and error. But however you choose to do it, you need to find a system. It's essential.

If you're struggling to manage your workload, organise your cage. Break things down. Look for common denominators. Create a system that works for you and implement it in all parts of your life. The more you keep doing this, the more you'll be able to focus. And the more you'll achieve.

LESSON 43

GAIN AN EDGE

More than anything, modern-day warfare is a mind-game.

As soldiers, a lot of our time was spent trying to gain an advantage over the enemy. By out-thinking them, or by playing them at their own game. Towards the end, it became like a gigantic high-stakes game of chess played out on the battlefield. We were constantly looking for an edge.

The truth is, there's only so much you can learn in combat training. There's a limit to how much weight you can carry on your backs. Your weaponry can only get so much more advanced. We don't even have the best hardware anymore: the Americans win hands-down on that front.

What separates us from other elite forces, what makes us without question *the* best fighting force in the world today, is our mindset.

In our teams, everyone has a voice. We're all ready and willing to share our opinions on how to get the job done. That's hugely important because we're all different. Each one of us brings a different perspective. We've all got different approaches to problem-solving. We're not limiting ourselves to a one-dimensional way of thinking.

Instead of going for the obvious solution, we're able to take a step back and think, 'How can we really put the bad guys on the back foot? How can we gain an edge over them here?'

As the old saying goes, there's more than one way to skin a cat. And as soldiers, that attitude gives us a huge advantage over our opponents. It means we're able to outwit the enemy. Time and again, throughout history, military forces that give everyone a voice and encourage people to question plans and decision-making have come out on top. They're able to stay one step ahead of the game.

This happens in the military all the time. A certain approach isn't getting the results you'd hoped for and everyone becomes frustrated. But instead of blindly sticking to the same tactics, we'll start talking among ourselves.

'We've got to be a bit sharper here, a bit more aware.' Discussing things. Finding a different solution that will allow us to outwit the bad guys. And more often than not, we'll get a different – and better – outcome. Because we're not afraid to mix things up, changing our tactics or adapting to the new situation on the ground.

This also unsettles the enemy. Being unpredictable and flexible in your approach means the other side can never rest easy, because they never know what to expect. It keeps them on their toes.

Don't blindly stick to the same tactics. When a particular approach to a problem stops working, look to mix things up. Draw on different voices in your team to find a new approach. When that happens, when you have multiple solutions on the board, you'll be able to stay one step ahead of the game.

THE SPARTANS AT THERMOPYLAE

The Spartans weren't unthinking warriors. They were intelligent fighters and masters at using the means at their disposal to gain an edge over their opponents.

During their training, the most promising Spartan youths were recruited to a secretive unit called the *Crypteria*. These lads were armed with daggers and given orders to sneak around the countryside, moving by night and laying up during the day, while terrorising the helots, a class of serf-like peasants forced to work the land for their Spartan masters. This ancient form of escape-and-evasion training taught the Spartans to study the land. To respect it. They learned how to fend off predators, how to move stealthily through the terrain. Most importantly, they learned how to make it work for them. In military campaigns, the *Crypteria* took on the role of a recce force, forward-mounting to covertly gather intel on the enemy.

When a huge Persian army under King Xerxes invaded Greece in 480 BC, about 4,000 Greek troops, including three hundred handpicked men from Sparta, went out to defend the pass at Thermopylae.

Thermopylae was a classic pinch point. The Spartans and their allies were facing an enemy host numbering a quarter of a million men, including the famous 'Immortals', crack troops from Xerxes's royal bodyguard. Their only hope of holding out against such a massive army was to hold a narrow path and act as a blocking force, denying the Persians the space to deploy their cavalry.

The path at Thermopylae, no more than ten metres wide, was flanked by marshland and the sea to the east, and steep mountains on its western side. There was a secret way around the pass, known to the locals, but the Spartans and their leader, Leonidas, were gambling that the Persians wouldn't know about it. As a precaution they posted a small force of about 1,000 men to guard the path – all Leonidas could spare from his small army.

The Persians waited four days at the pass, expecting – or hoping – that the defenders would roll over. But Leonidas and his men were resolute. When a Persian scout was sent forward to get eyeballs on the defenders, he saw a group of Spartan warriors combing their hair and calmly going through their daily exercise routines. This is a great example of gaining an edge: through their actions the Spartans were sending a very clear message to the enemy. *We're here*, they were saying. *We're not going anywhere. We're not afraid.*

On the fifth day Xerxes gave the order to advance.

For two long days the Persians unsuccessfully attacked the pass. The Spartans were experienced soldiers, whereas the

Persian troops were levies drawn from a multitude of nations, each with different languages and ways of fighting. On a few occasions the Spartans used the old trick of pretending to turn and flee; as soon as the Persians gave chase they would swing round and cut down the onrushing rabble.

After the first attacks were repulsed Xerxes threw his Immortals into the contest, but they also failed to make any headway against the close ranks of the Spartans. The defenders guarded against fatigue by rotating their troops, with one group fighting while the other guys recovered.

On the second night, the Persians learned about the goat path leading around the pass. Xerxes sent a body of men to cross the path at night-time. Early the next morning they routed the small force guarding the path and swooped down towards the remaining Spartan defenders, intending to attack them from the rear.

Trapped between enemy forces in front and at his rear, Leonidas took the decision to send away some of the Greeks, probably because he feared they might flee in disorder anyway, once they realised they were doomed, which would negatively impact on the morale of his men.

Most of the Spartans' allies departed for their home cities. The Spartans themselves stayed behind with their king and prepared to fight to the death. They rushed out of the narrows and met the enemy at a wider section of the road. Some of the Persians were trampled to death during the fighting by their own sides; others were driven into the sea and drowned. At some point in the battle Leonidas was killed. The surviving Spartans fought over their king's body and pulled back to a small hill to make a final stand. They fought on like animals, using their bare hands and even their teeth, until they were finally cut down by Persian archers.

By maximising the environment and their resources, the Spartans had resisted a much, much stronger enemy for three days. They had shown the Persians that they wouldn't have things their own way from now on. That they were prepared to fight to the death. And in doing so they set an example to the rest of Greece.

Whatever the task in front of you – whatever the odds you face – think like the Spartans at the Hot Gates. Always look to gain a decisive edge.

- Learn to distinguish between those things you can control, and those things outside your influence. Remember: if the mortars are raining down on you in the desert, there's nothing you can do about it – so don't waste your time worrying.

- Fear can only be controlled by consistently exposing yourself to it. When you repeatedly commit to confronting fear, you'll experience the amazing benefits of achievement and reward. You'll make fear work for you.

- Turn down the volume on your negative thoughts. Instead of asking yourself, 'What if I fall?' ask yourself, 'What if I *don't*?'

- The hardest path is always the most rewarding. When you're tempted to take the path of least resistance, tell yourself that the hardest route is the only one available. And start moving.

- Every obstacle can be overcome or navigated around. The key is to arm yourself with information on the hurdle. Then you'll find the best way to get round, over, under or through it.

- Be forward thinking in your daily life. Avoid reaching for the easy or lazy solution. Look at the situation and think ahead.

- Practise emotional adaptability. Analyse your emotions and thought processes when you commit to actions. Understanding the power of mind over body is the key to recovering from setbacks.

- Compartmentalise and break things down. Organise your things. A physically ordered environment goes hand-in-hand with an organised mind.

- Always look to stay ahead of the game. Bring in other voices and look at multiple solutions. A small edge can be the difference between success and failure.

PART SIX

LEADERSHIP AND TEAMWORK

LESSON 44

COMMUNICATE EFFECTIVELY

Good teamwork begins with good communication.

Soldiers spend a lot of time together, so we know each other inside out. We know what makes our pals tick. How they operate on the battlefield. Where they keep their kit. Everything, right down to the tiniest detail.

This is important, because it's not always possible to communicate verbally in the combat zone. It might only be a look, a hand signal, or some other gesture. And the reverse is true too. Your mate might not be able to tell you that something is up, but if you really know them well, you'll be able to figure this out just from observing their gait, the way they're moving in combat, or the way they've walked into training that day.

Whether it's spoken or unspoken, being able to communicate clearly with that person is a massive part of creating a good team. It's the ability to let your mates know that you've got their back, *no matter what.*

Effective communication goes hand-in-hand with professionalism. You might not get on with your colleague outside

273

of the battlefield, or the workplace, but if you're a top professional, any personal animosity that may exist, or petty grievances or mutual dislike – all of that goes straight out of the window. As soon as you're on the job, it becomes one hundred per cent unconditional commitment to each other.

We're almost like brothers in the military, with all the messiness, friendship and squabbles that entails. We hate each other one minute, love each other the next. But when you go into a combat zone, you switch. You set your differences aside, and it becomes about unconditional commitment to one another.

Trust is equally important in cultivating good communication. How well you communicate depends on the strength of the bond between you and your pals, how fortified that level of trust is within your unit, or team.

When you establish that bond, you realise that a massive part of good communication isn't actually down to you. It's about your mates, and their ability to identify when you need help. When they need to bail you out.

The purest form of communication is when you don't need to ask for help. Instead, your muckers are there straight away. Because they know if something isn't right. But that can only happen when there's a tight bond between everyone on the team.

That's what makes a highly effective team. When you know each other so well that you don't need to communicate verbally. The unspoken becomes as powerful as the spoken. It doesn't have to be a complicated gesture. It might be as simple as someone reaching out and squeezing your shoulder – as happened to me on one occasion, when I found myself frozen with fear.

Every soldier experiences fear at some point, because it's a hugely powerful emotion. Maybe the most powerful of all. Which means it is sometimes out of your control, despite all your training and experience, and no matter how hard you try to control it, or how many times you've found yourself in the same situation in the past. You can't help feeling that way. It's an instinctive reaction, and it gets all of us sooner or later. In any threatening or dangerous situation, you've got the options of fight, flight or freeze. Most of the time, as highly trained soldiers, we're going to be fight. But there are times when freeze will win out. Which is what happened to me. I was rooted to the spot, gripped with fear.

At that moment of crisis, one of the lads squeezed my shoulder. It was a small gesture, but it spoke volumes. It was my mucker's way of reassuring me. He knew I had been seized by fear. That squeeze told me not to worry. That he had my back, no matter what.

As soon as he squeezed my shoulder, something strange happened. Even now, I find it hard to describe. It felt like everything left my body. All my fears and emotions, all the things that had kept me from moving through that doorway. I felt as light as a feather. All of a sudden I was able to push past the fear and get on with the mission.

Later on, I told my mucker I was sorry for freezing during the mission. He just looked at me.

'What are you talking about, mate?' he asked.

'I've never done that before,' I explained. 'Freezing like that. I don't know what happened.'

He threw back his head and laughed it off, and we all had a joke about it. But that's the importance of being honest in your communication. If I hadn't brought that incident up with Steve, if I'd tried to brush it under the carpet, my mucker probably would have brought it up with me instead. Asked me if I was alright. And I could have shrugged it off. Made light of it. Come back with some crap excuse.

But he didn't need to say anything. Because I'd been open with him. He could laugh it off, because he knew that, in my own way, I was thanking him for what he'd done.

You don't always have to say what's on your mind to make yourself understood. Sometimes you don't need to say anything at all. What's left unspoken can be just as powerful as what's said out loud.

After that incident I felt so good about what had happened that I started feeling invincible. That wasn't down to me: it was the team that gave me that sense of invincibility, knowing that I had those guys at my side. That was due to the high level of communication we had between us. The honesty and trust within the group. Whenever we went on a mission, we all knew that no matter what happened, we had each other's backs. *We've got this.* That can have a powerful impact in terms of enhancing team performance.

That bond can only be built patiently, brick by brick, with trust. Trust comes from honest and pure communication. And when you know you can communicate *without communicating* – without saying anything – then as a team you're laughing. You'll feel like nothing can stop you. You'll create an unstoppable team.

'It is of immense importance that the soldier, high or low, whatever rank he has, should not have to encounter in War those things which, when seen for the first time, set him in astonishment and perplexity; if he has only met with them one single time before, even by that he is half acquainted with them. This relates even to bodily fatigues. They should be practised less to accustom the body to them than the mind.'

Carl von Clausewitz, On War, Book I, Chapter 8

LESSON 45

SING FROM THE SAME HYMN SHEET

To an outsider the unique – and sometimes brutal – ways of army life can be hard to understand.

During my early days in the military I'd sometimes wake up and find that my bed had been tipped upside down. Geezers might punch you in the middle of the night for a laugh. Other times I'd come back from leave and discover that my locker had been trashed, or my room had been smashed up.

In the Royal Marines, new recruits used to take part in what was called a joining run. They'd have to participate in roll-mat fights, which involved all the new blokes wrapping a couple of sleeping mats over their arms and having a big free-for-all in a makeshift arena. Last man standing wins. Those fights were hardcore. You'd have guys getting clotheslined, people getting knocked out. At the end of it the winner would stand in front of the cheering onlookers and pump his arms in the air, blood all over the place.

One of the exercises on the joining runs involved jumping completely naked out of a window and landing in a bramble bush. This might appear pointless and unnecessarily painful. And don't get me wrong, it did hurt like hell. But it also teaches you a lesson. There's no point trying to carefully extract yourself from a thick bramble. It's going to hurt you either way.

So your best bet is to rush out as fast as you can. Get it over and done with. When you run out of the bush, the thorns tearing at your skin, everyone cheering you on, blood dripping down your body, you're actually being taught a valuable lesson. It makes you understand the Marines' ethos. 'Get in there and get the job done. Don't mess about because that is only going to prolong the suffering. If you're going to do something, then push through the pain and get on with it.'

This sort of stuff might sound like a culture of bullying. And don't get me wrong, in some cases it probably *was* taken too far. But I personally never thought of it that way. That stuff played an important role in moulding us into warriors. Conditioning us, body and mind. It taught us to harden ourselves.

It was almost like the guys in the unit were putting up two fingers to the initial training routines. Telling the military system, 'You think what you've just pushed us through is hard? Think again. Look at what we can force upon ourselves. What we've endured in training is *nothing* compared to this.'

These activities also served another purpose, though. In a messed-up kind of way, they helped to create a team bond. That might be hard for some people to accept. But that doesn't make it any less true.

The joining runs were the Troop's own way of welcoming you to the unit – to your new military family. Each activity created a spirit of camaraderie between the new guys and the established soldiers.

At the end of it all, once it's done, you're sitting round together with the old sweats, drinking beer and having a laugh, even though you might be bleeding from your arms and legs, or you've taken a beating in the roll-mat scrap. Then a few months later the next batch of recruits come in and you've got another joining run, and the lads that have done it previously are now the ones running the show.

There were other things that could make your life uncomfortable or even miserable. Certain codes that shaped the values and ethos of the different units.

In the airborne units, for example, using a weapon sling was seen as a sign of weakness. This created some truly ridiculous situations. We'd be tabbing across the training area in Sennybridge, the lads lugging their General-Purpose Machine Gun (GPMG) with the weapon sling attached. The GPMGs are big, heavy units, so while no one was looking they'd use the slings. Then someone would see another patrol approaching with a different cap badge. All of a sudden there was a mad scramble to take the slings off before the other unit caught up with them.

The patrol would go past the other group, the lads straining under the weight of their de-slung GPMGs. Like a bunch of macho idiots.

Then there was the question of whether you were allowed a dessert – what was known in the Royal Marines as a 'duff'. In 9 Parachute Squadron we used to share the scoff house with other ranks and cap badges. But in the Marines, if you were airborne – if you had parachute wings – you weren't allowed to eat any dessert. If someone saw you eating duff in the scoff house, and you had your airborne wings, you'd get a lashing on your arse with a stable belt.

Miserable as it sounds, all this stuff helped create an individual team ethos. The values for each unit or squadron were different, and the attitudes varied too. You were expected to carry yourself in a different way in 9 Parachute Squadron compared with, say, the Royal Marines.

If you didn't fit in, the experience could be brutal. It was very much a case of either you adhere to it and embrace the ethos or get lost. But it worked. It meant that everyone in the unit had the same mindset. A shared mentality. It was how we defined ourselves.

We were all singing from the same hymn sheet.

From the moment you volunteer to join a particular unit, whether it's in logistics, engineers, signallers, you're being told, 'This is who we are. This is what we're about. This is what makes us the most credible force in the whole military.'

In the conventional forces you've got all these subdivisions, each moulding their recruits from a young age, when they're most impressionable, to believe that they're the very best. In that situation, you're going to have intense competition, and your team will perform better as a result.

If you want to build or improve morale in your team, create a unique ethos. Make sure that everyone is singing off the same hymn sheet. When your group has a shared ethos, they won't just be working towards the goal or cause. They'll be working for each other. A team with that mindset is always going to perform.

KING SHAKA, MILITARY GENIUS OF THE ZULUS

Before Shaka came to power in 1816, Zulu warfare was low-level stuff, fought between the different clans. Warriors spent most of their time living in military camps called 'kraals'. They served alongside other Zulus in their age-group and spent much of their time policing their chief's territory and maintaining the royal herd. Wars were small in scale and didn't last long. The clans would meet at a pre-agreed time and place and chuck spears at each other until one group lost its nerve.

Shaka changed all of that. He knew from his own fighting experience that the key to creating a strong army was to get the men to be dedicated and committed to each other, rather than their clan or tribe. So he tore up the rule book. He got rid of the old way of organising the warriors and formed the men into brand-new regiments, each with its own unique identity. There was a regiment for married men and one for bachelors. There was even a group of herdboys, younger and therefore more impressionable than some of the veterans.

These units were given their own distinctive uniform and colour-coded shields. They even had their own battle cries and war songs.

Life as a Zulu warrior was hardcore. They trained in drills and manoeuvres and carried out route marches of up to sixty miles a day while barefoot. Anyone who failed to keep up was executed on the spot. Every man was expected to kill in battle. Those who failed to do so or lost their spears in the fighting were condemned as cowards and put to death.

These changes encouraged a fierce competitive spirit between the regiments, to the point where their camps had to be sited far apart from one another to avoid coming to blows. This helped to boost discipline and maintain standards in the ranks – because now every warrior had a duty to uphold the reputation of his unit. The clan loyalties were replaced by something far stronger. Now the Zulu warrior's loyalty was first and foremost to his regiment – and to Shaka.

With a ruthlessly disciplined and well-drilled force at his disposal Shaka set about expanding his kingdom. By the time of his death he commanded an army of more than 20,000 hardened warriors and ruled over an area of about 200,000 square kilometres.

Even after his death in 1828, Shaka's influence loomed large over the Zulu army. In 1879, during the Anglo-Zulu War, a force of Zulu warriors, fighting in Shaka's bull-horn formation, crushed the British at the Battle of Isandlwana – a victory that astonished the world.

Shaka's achievements bear comparison with the best generals in history. But none of it would have been possible without the spirit of camaraderie he created among his men. The Zulu warriors' unquestioning loyalty and dedication to their regiments, to each other – and their king – helped to lay the groundwork for Shaka's extraordinary victories.

LESSON 46
SEEK GOOD FOLLOWSHIP

A good leader, in any walk of life, shouldn't be satisfied with simply leading or mentoring their team. A leader should aim to have the people below them want to take their position. Good leaders should aim for *good followship*. Followship is when you want to take that leadership position from someone. By this I don't mean cynically eyeing up your boss's role because you think you know better than them. Followship is something *positive*. It happens when you want to know everything that's going on, when you're hungry to find out more about the team leader and their responsibilities. How they work.

A leader achieves this by empowering their team. When you do that, as a leader, people will naturally want to work for you, because they can see that you're putting everything into training them. You're investing in your team.

Most people don't think about followship. They obsess over leadership, but the truth is, you can't have good leadership without having good followship. That means not hiding anything from your team. Leading from the front, rather than trying to command from the rear echelon. It means not dishing out orders without giving context. It means genuinely having the best interests of your team at heart. Caring for the welfare of your soldiers, wanting them to better themselves, to learn and grow.

Followship is how you know if you're a good leader or not. It's not someone telling you, 'Mate, you're a really great boss.' It's having good fellowship. When you bring the team into the decision-making process, they feel validated. They feel worthy.

To do that, when you take up a leadership position you need to leave your ego at the door. You need to be willing to be accountable to the people on your team, to go to them when you're struggling, or when you've made a mistake.

My first tour in Afghanistan really threw this lesson into focus. I went out as the 2iC within my eight-man section, under the leadership of the section commander. When you have a contact with the enemy, the section breaks down into two four-man fire teams. The 2iC leads one team; the section commander takes charge of the other fire team, while also staying in overall charge of the whole group. You need to master a whole different skillset when you're a section commander: orders processes, map-reading and so on. The responsibility is much greater.

Two weeks into our tour, our Troop Sergeant was sent home to deal with a family emergency. My section commander stepped up into the position of Troop Sergeant; as 2iC I got bumped up to section commander. At the time

I was only a Lance Corporal, a fairly lowly rank. A section commander will normally hold the rank of Corporal, which could have put me at a disadvantage. But as 2iC I had always paid close attention to everything that was going on around me. I had studied my section commander. My mindset was very much: *I want that guy's job.* I was very confident in my map-reading, in my ability to deliver an orders process. Even if I didn't always get it right. When the position came up, I wanted that extra responsibility. I was happy to take on that challenge.

As a section commander, I went from being in charge of three other guys to leading seven guys – eight, including myself. With eight men you can cause some serious damage: you've got a tremendous amount of firepower and manpower at your disposal, a ton of equipment. You have a responsibility not only to you and your muckers, but also to the hardware you're carrying – and we carried a *lot* of stuff. As a section commander you're accountable for all of it.

The section commander is also responsible for navigation on the ground. That's a whole challenge by itself – as I found out the hard way.

It happened on my third or fourth mission in charge. We were on the ground, navigating through a typical Afghan landscape: a patchwork of square fields bordered by irrigation ditches, with a much bigger central ditch running through the area, which we'd use to take cover. Every so often we'd emerge from the ditch and cross a path, staying on the outskirts of the villages. These were hearts-and-minds ops, intended to win over the villagers to our side, so we took great care to avoid disturbing the locals unless there were clear signs of Taliban activity.

We dipped out of a ditch and came upon a built-up area. Lots of compounds. I moved down a series of alleyways, trying to find my way back to the outskirts of the village, but instead I seemed to be moving deeper and deeper into the settlement. It started getting eerie. The place was deserted. The shops – really just a handful of mud huts with corrugated iron roofs – were all closed, which was another bad sign.

After we had passed several compounds, I thought, 'I've got to call this.'

I stopped at a cross-alley. Knelt down. Called the lads over. 'Close in, close in,' I said.

They gathered round. Everyone was on high-alert. We formed all-round defence, covering all the angles.

One of the guys said, in a low whisper, 'What's up, Ant?'

'I'm bloody lost, lads,' I said.

Everyone burst into laughter. 'We were wondering where you were going,' someone else replied, grinning broadly, taking the edge off the situation. The tension drained away.

After we'd had a good laugh, we collectively came together and got our bearings. 'This is where you went wrong,' another guy explained, pointing to an area of the map. 'You crossed this field too soon. You should have carried on for another two fields before cutting back in.'

That's the sign of a good leader. Admitting when you're wrong. Being able to put aside your ego for the good of the team.

I didn't have to tell the lads I was lost. I could have pushed on, past another three or four compounds, pretended that I knew where I was going. But that mentality might have resulted in the whole section being killed. We could have been ambushed or blundered into an IED. Any number of things might have happened.

Sometimes you just have to swallow your pride.

When we got back to the FOB (Forward Operating Base), the other lads predictably gave me hell. They used to nickname me 'Atlas' because of my strength; now they started calling me 'Mapless'. Fair play. I deserved it. But after two or three days, the jokes stopped – because I'd held myself accountable.

Consider what might have happened if I hadn't admitted my mistake during the patrol. If I had let pride and ego win, and accidentally led us into an ambush. That would have stayed with me throughout the rest of my military career. But because I'd held up my hands and reached out to my teammates, they were in a position to think, 'Wow, the section commander is coming to us for help. We're worth something. We're valuable. Together we can get out of anything.'

I didn't grasp the significance of this lesson until a few months later. I was reviewing my past performance. Critically assessing how I'd carried myself on previous ops. Looking back at the good, the bad and the ugly, asking myself what I could have done better, or differently.

When I reviewed this incident, I suddenly realised that this had been a valuable leadership lesson. Not being afraid to go to your team and say, 'I've done something wrong here.'

By admitting my error to my muckers, I had shown that I respected their opinions.

Hold up your hands when you've blundered, or when you're unsure about something. When you do that, you're collectively encouraging the team to work together to get out of trouble. You're *leading* in the most complete sense of the word.

I put this into practice during my time as section commander with the Royal Marines. I'd stop in the middle of an operation, get the guys to gather round, and stab a finger at the map.

'Right, this is us,' I'd begin, tracing my finger across the map. 'We need to get all the way over here. This is the route I was planning on taking. Should we take another route? Does anyone have any thoughts or suggestions about this?'

The team would study the route. Then I'd suggest clearing another area. 'We could go up that way, but if there's trouble then we're going to have to pull back a short distance to here. If you're happy with that, we can go through this new area. Or we can leave it for today. Talk about it after the mission and venture off in that direction tomorrow. What do you think?'

I was bringing them into the decision-making process.

As section commander I felt it was my responsibility to focus on the more experienced guys, the ones who would want to take my job one day. That's part and parcel of military life. If anything happens to me on the battlefield, somebody else needs to step up there and then. In the combat zone, there's no time to post a job advert and interview candidates. So I worked a bit closer with those guys. I didn't exclude the younger ones – that would have been poor leadership

– but I wanted the more experienced ones to feel validated. To want to step into my boots.

When you do this, the other members of your team will want to work for you, because you're giving them respect. A sense of self-worth. You're letting them know that their opinions matter. You're creating a tight bond.

That attitude filters down to the rest of the team. The new 2iC will give special attention to those guys who might want to step up and become Lance Corporal, for example. You create a culture of followship throughout the team. That is how you get the best out of people.

When you don't have followship, people are going to feel less invested in the mission. They might switch off. It's easy to stand at the back of the patrol, not being proactive, happy to follow on. But when everyone is made to feel equal, whatever their role on the team, they will start to believe they're capable of doing great things.

LEADERSHIP, IN WHATEVER FIELD, SHOULD BE ABOUT TEACHING THE PEOPLE AROUND YOU WHAT THEY NEED TO KNOW IN ORDER TO TAKE OVER YOUR ROLE, BY PUTTING CONTROL IN THEIR HANDS. RELINQUISHING RESPONSIBILITY: THAT'S WHAT BEING A LEADER REALLY MEANS.

The ability to say to your team, 'You're in control of this now. I trust you.' Your team members, in turn, will feel like they've achieved something. They'll start to tell themselves, 'Yes. I can do this. I've contributed something valuable to the team. I want to learn more, achieve more.'

Leadership, in whatever field, should be about teaching the people around you what they need to know in order to take over your role, by putting control in their hands. Relinquishing responsibility: that's what being a leader really means.

There's another benefit to this approach: it will also help to grow the person occupying the leadership role. They can learn from their teaching experiences, understand how to instruct people more effectively, improving their personal development – which in turn will help them go up to the next level on the career ladder. It's a win-win.

If you're in a leadership position, ask yourself: 'How do I lead? Am I making sure that everyone on the team has a voice, an opinion? Am I bringing people together and getting them to collaborate and share ideas?'

Never underestimate the power of good followship. The greater your followship, the more you consult your team members, the more they will want to contribute, and the more options you'll have on the table. And the more likely you are to complete the mission.

If you're struggling to motivate the people in your team, look inwards before you begin questioning their dedication. Ask yourself if you've laid the foundations to create good followship. Without followship you cannot have effective leadership.

'The art of Life is more like that of the wrestler than of the dancer; for the wrestler must always be ready on his guard, and stand firm against the sudden, unforeseen efforts of his adversary.'

Marcus Aurelius, Meditations, Book 7.61

HAVE THE COURAGE TO ASK

In the military, you learn to break things down to the lowest common denominator. Reduce them to their most fundamental level, so that everyone on your team fully understands the plan. This is critical to mission success. It's no use if the lads only grasp eighty or even ninety per cent of the op: if you don't fully understand something, you can't process it.

It's down to you, as the individual soldier, to break down a plan, until you fully comprehend it. If you don't do that, you won't be able to move on. Even if you do try to move on, it's pointless, because you're going to come unstuck sooner or later. How are you meant to action something when you only understand ninety per cent of it? You're not going to achieve what you set out to do.

To succeed at anything in life, you need to ask questions. As a soldier I embraced that attitude constantly, because we're dealing with high-stakes situations and mistakes can lead to serious injury or death.

If you're not sure about something, or you don't ask that

burning question, you're starting off from a position of weakness. You're only going to know eighty per cent of the plan, which means you're going to have twenty per cent of uncertainty floating about in your head. You'll fall at the final hurdle because you won't have fully understood the process. You'll find yourself faced with a solid wall instead of a door. Then you're in trouble.

You have to recognise the importance of fully grasping a plan. Tell yourself, 'I need to know what is going on at all times.' By breaking things down, you'll completely understand every aspect of the process.

There's a good example of this. I was doing a mission briefing.

We had some lads from another team joining us on this particular op. As I outlined the plan, I could see one of the younger guys from this unit frowning. In a way he reminded me of myself.

When I had finished this guy had the courage to stick up his hand and admit that he didn't understand part of the briefing. He wanted clarification.

I looked at this lad and thought, 'Wow. That's exactly the sort of question I would have asked if I was in his position.' Because I had neglected to break things down to the bare minimum for the guys from the other unit. That was my mistake.

It would have been easy for this guy to stay silent, even though he didn't have an understanding of the mission details. But instead of worrying about looking like an idiot, this guy had dared to ask the question. He wanted to have the full picture in his head: the help that was available to us, the different units that would have our backs if things went wrong or the plan changed.

From the expression on his face, I could see that the penny had dropped. 'Got it, Ant,' he said. This guy wasn't satisfied with just knowing his own role. He wanted to comprehend the bigger picture. He wanted to know the workings of the entire military machine involved in that operation. That's golden.

Everyone involved in the job should be aware of every aspect of it, right down to the smallest detail. Yes, you're going to do your bit, but it's not enough just to know your own role. You need to understand what else is going on, when and how and why. The ins and outs. The whole package.

That applies to other walks of life too. If you action something without fully understanding it, you're either going to do it badly, or you won't see the action through. Because at a certain point you'll come up against something you don't grasp, and you won't feel confident about performing the rest of the job. Then you're much more likely to throw in the towel. Or you have to retrace your steps. Work your way back to an earlier stage and try to understand where you went wrong. Where you need to go.

Be a courageous questioner. Before you undertake any task or company project, have the courage to ask yourself, 'What don't I know? What don't I understand?' Break down even the smallest thing until you know you've completely got it.

BUILD A CONSISTENT TEAM

A good leader has to know their team inside out.

In my team, I embraced that attitude to the maximum. I made it my business to find out everything about my muckers. What made them tick. Whether they were emotional, or headstrong, or their own worst critic.

Elite soldiers spend more time with their teammates than they do with anyone else. When you get to know your pals really well, you'll learn to recognise their *disconnects*. What I mean by this is situations when consistency in the performance of one or more of your teammates breaks down.

Consistency is the key to any successful team. If you have a group of individuals who are consistently good at their jobs and perform to a high level, then you're going to be able to identify when something goes wrong. If one of your mates is having an off-day, or they're distracted, there will be a slight but noticeable drop in standards.

Individual consistency comes from all three strands of the Trilogy – the physical, the emotional and the psychological.

Physical consistency relates to your fitness. Your overall health. What you put into your body, how hard you train. The psychological component involves being mentally stable, having a mental fortress, not a prison. Consistency of emotions means you're able to stay level-headed in new and unfamiliar situations; your responses to situations don't fluctuate dramatically.

The Consistency Trilogy is essential for any branch of the military. If you're disciplined in yourself, and consistent in all aspects of the Trilogy, then you're going to be an excellent all-round soldier.

This also carries another benefit. Because if you're working with highly consistent individual team members, you'll know when someone is distracted, or having a bad day. Their standards will drop, even if it's only by a fraction. The tell-tale signs will be obvious to you because you'll know your teammates. And you'll be able to identify the disconnect.

One of my best pals in the military was emotionally cut off. A closed book. Emotions never came into play for him. He was the opposite of an emotional individual – this guy was an ox. Super-reliable and consistent in his attitude. He'd show up at training every single day. But he tended to overthink. I knew that. I *knew* him. I could tell when he was distracted just by looking him in the eye.

Whenever this guy was having an off-day, I knew he had to be distracted by something in his head. The disconnect would be psychological. It wouldn't be an emotional issue, and it wasn't a physical drop in his standards. On those occasions I'd ask him, 'What's distracting you, mate? What are you worried about?'

Sure enough, the problem would be a case of overthinking something. A mental break. It might be trying to identify a position on a map, or figuring out how to do an orders process.

That's teamwork. Understanding your muckers, learning everything about them. Getting the best out of each other, so your teammates can be the best version of themselves. Perhaps one of your colleagues is mentally very strong but has a habit of getting a bit emotional. I've known guys like that in my military career. Top soldiers, but in certain situations they can end up letting their emotions take control of them. They end up making decisions based on emotion, rather than assessing the situation from a coldly logical point of view.

In the military sphere, that kind of disconnect is dangerous. It can endanger a mission, and maybe the lives of your muckers. But whatever the situation, if you know your teammates really well, you can immediately pinpoint the disconnect and help them get back that consistency wavelength.

It's not necessarily about your colleagues making the wrong decision, either. This isn't about apportioning blame. But the success of the overall task or business objective or mission should always be at the forefront of your thinking. Whenever you identify or recognise a disconnect it's important to ask yourself, 'How can I maximise my pals in order to maximise the team's capability, so we can get this job done as fast and efficiently as possible?'

When someone on your sports team or in the workplace suffers an emotional disconnect, here's what happens. Percentage points are being taken away from that person's performance. What you need to do is top them back up. Repair that disconnect. It doesn't matter if it's someone senior to you – if you see a disconnect happening, you need to take matters into your own hands. Make that decision for the good of the team.

This happened to me multiple times in my career in the military. There have been occasions when I've paused for too long on a mission and someone had to give me a nudge or a pat on the shoulder. Or I've been too keen to get on with something. One of the lads might tell me, 'Ant, let's just wait a bit. You're going to run into a suicide mission, for Christ's sake.'

These disconnects can manifest themselves in various ways. Maybe it's physical. Maybe not hitting the gym every day, or you're not dedicating yourself to doing your military fitness. We used to work out for two hours each morning before the day even began. One of the lads couldn't be bothered to do this. But then we'd be running onto the target, carrying all of our kit, and when we'd hit the front of the compound we'd still be waiting for that bloke to catch up. Someone will take that guy to the side, back at camp. Have a word. 'Mate, you need to sort your phys out. Get it sorted.'

Or it could be that someone's head isn't in the game. Maybe they're distracted. Maybe there's something going on at home. In which case you need to give them some tough love. 'I don't care if your missus has just dumped you, that's not my problem. All I need to know is this: is your head in the game? Are you ready? Because if not we'll send you home and put a battlefield replacement in your place.'

Sometimes we wouldn't have the freedom or liberty to replace people. In those instances, all you can do is put them in a different role. Stick them somewhere they're least likely to impact negatively on the team.

In the military, you don't have time to go round dealing

with everyone's problems. That's not your job. But equally, you don't want to go on a mission with a mate who's looking distracted, for example. Because if you know or suspect something is up with that person, and you don't do anything about it – if something happens to them on the mission, you're going to feel supremely bad. Guilt will kick in.

Find the time to talk it through with them before things go wrong. If someone on my team is acting a bit weird, or if they're distracted because of a situation at home, the best thing to do is talk about it. I'm not saying that will clear that person's mind or remove the distraction completely. But if I can strip it back, return a couple of percentage points to that person, so that they feel a bit better about themselves, and more confident, they're obviously going to perform better.

It's not about the individual. It's about the overall performance of the team. That must always be the leader's priority. If you can make people feel better about themselves, or lighten the burden they're carrying around, you're going to enhance the team.

In the military doing this is an absolute must because you're placing your life in your mate's hands. But the same applies to any group, whether it's a sports team, or your colleagues in the workplace.

Disconnects are going to happen. Somewhere along the line, on the battleground, someone is going to experience a problem. Percentage points are going to be stripped from either you or one of your muckers. It's the nature of the beast. What matters then is how you and your mates react in that situation.

If you're struggling to deal with a difficult team member, try to get to know them better. Try to understand what makes them tick. When you do that, you'll be able to identify the root cause of their unhappiness or discontent and work to address it.

LESSON 49

GET EVERYONE PULLING
IN THE SAME DIRECTION

Over time, the idea of what makes mission success has evolved.

It used to be accepted wisdom that the mission always came first. 'No one is more important than the mission,' so the saying went. But that's not really true. You *are* bigger than the op, in fact, because I need you for the next one, and the one after that.

Success isn't about whether we take down the bad guys or not. It's about the team coming back fully intact, with everyone alive and well. Not being reckless while we're on the ground, not putting each other at risk. Looking out for one another. Being dedicated to each other.

Making sure we're all pulling in the same direction.

Perhaps one of my pals is taking incoming rounds from the left flank. We're not going to leave him to sort out his problem on his own while we move forward to capture the target. All we're going to do is create a disconnect in the team. He might get injured or killed, and then we're in serious trouble. Instead, let's pause the mission, peel off from the main target and deal with the situation on the flank. Help out our mucker. Then we can swing round and get back onto the actual mission.

The mission, whatever form it takes, is the easy part. Looking after each other, working together, making your cause *each other* – that's much harder to achieve. But when everyone is pulling in the same direction, you and your team-mates will feel unstoppable.

XENOPHON AND THE
TEN THOUSAND

In 401 BC, an army of 10,000 Greek mercenaries was hired by Cyrus the Younger to help him claim the Persian throne from his older brother. But when Cyrus was killed in battle near Babylon, the Greeks found themselves stranded, far from their homeland, surrounded on all sides by hostile forces, in a land they did not know. To make matters worse a number of their leaders had been taken prisoner by the Persians, tortured and put to death.

The Greek warriors, battle-scarred veterans of the Peloponnesian War, had a simple choice. They could stay put and surrender, in which case they would probably meet the same fate as the dead commanders. They could fight, but they would eventually be overrun and captured or killed. Or they could return home. They could get up, organise themselves and begin the long walk east towards the Black Sea.

They chose to march.

Ahead of them was a 1,000-mile journey through an unfamiliar landscape, with the men forced to live off the land and harassed by enemy forces every step of the way. They had to fight their way across mountain passes and cross rivers defended by hordes of enemy warriors. In Armenia they faced snowstorms and hunger and attacks from raiding parties. The men suffered appallingly from frostbite and snow-blindness. Only when they caught sight of the Black Sea, a few days' march from Trebizond, did the Greeks finally know they were safe.

The Ten Thousand survived these ordeals partly because of their training and fighting experience. These were tough men. But more importantly, they worked as a team, holding councils of war and assemblies to discuss their situation and bring together different voices and points of view. In this way they gave themselves multiple options to solve each problem they faced on the long journey home. They were all pulling in the same direction.

One episode illustrates this perfectly. The Greeks had reached the Botan River, on the border between Armenia and the land of the Carduchians. An initial attempt to ford the river had to be aborted because it was too difficult. At dawn they discovered a force of Armenian mercenaries forming up on the far bank. Meanwhile a body of Carduchian troops had gathered at their rear, ready to cut them to pieces the moment they tried to cross the Botan.

One of the leaders of these warriors was a Greek noble called Xenophon. He was approached at breakfast by two young warriors. They told Xenophon they had discovered a second, secret fordable point on the river by chance while out gathering wood for a fire.

But even with the knowledge of the ford, the Ten Thousand were not yet safe. They still had to get around the other major problem: what to do about the enemy forces on both sides of the river. If they tried to cross at one point, the Armenians would be waiting for them on the other side.

Xenophon's solution was to divide the Greek army into two. Half the men made for the second fording point, with the rest staying behind with Xenophon. While the first force made its way across, Xenophon raced back to the original crossing point with the rest of the men, tricking the enemy into thinking he planned to get across there and attack the enemy in the flank. This had the effect of drawing enemy troops away from the secret ford further along the river.

Once he was sure this was working Xenophon then hurried back over to cover the rest of the men crossing the Botan. By now the Carduchian warriors were pouring down from the slopes onto the plain, threatening the baggage train and the camp followers at the rear of the Greek force.

Xenophon and his men held their position until the others had successfully crossed the Botan. The Carduchians, realising that only a small force remained on the near bank, advanced towards the Greeks, loosing slingshot and arrows. The Greeks waited for a pause in the barrage. Then they charged at the enemy.

As soon as the Carduchians saw what was happening they panicked, turned and bolted across the plain. At that moment the trumpeter sounded the signal, the Greeks called off their pursuit and scrambled across the river as fast as their legs could carry them, covered by a throng of javelin-throwers and archers who'd entered the water on the far side.

This is a brilliant example of teamwork in a crisis. The Ten Thousand had no option but to rely on each other if they were going to stay alive. Everyone was striving towards the same goal: survival. My life depends on your life and vice versa. That's what got the Greeks through their numerous ordeals. They put aside their discrepancies and worked towards the common goal, the most important one of all: life itself. And they knew they were stronger together.

Teamwork isn't just about the military or the workplace. The most important team is the family. That's where teamwork really begins. Everything spreads outwards from there. Because ultimately, all teams are about caring for people. If you can crack that team at home, you'll find it easier to master teamwork in a social circle or with your colleagues at work. You'll be able to dig deeper and work even harder to achieve your goal together – as the Ten Thousand did on their epic journey back home.

'A strong mind is one which does not lose its balance even under the most violent excitement.'

Carl von Clausewitz, On War, Book I, Chapter 3

LESSON 50

BE A LEADER IN YOUR OWN LIFE

You don't have to be in a leadership position to be a leader.

If you've got your life in order, if you're showing consistency in your discipline, if you're organised in body and mind, if you're going to work and your head is in the game – then you're leading. You're demonstrating leadership in *your own life*.

In the military, the guy who puts in a couple of hours in the gym before training each day – he's leadership material. He's showing discipline. That guy is leading his own life the best way he knows how, and he's succeeding. He's a potential leader. If I'm looking to send someone on a leadership course, that's who I'm choosing.

A clean locker is another tell-tale sign of a soldier with good leadership in their own life. Some guys, they come in and their locker looks scruffy, they look untidy in their personal appearance. That person hasn't got their own house in order. Whereas someone who irons his kit properly, whacks on his boots, keeps his locker tidy and is never late – you know that person is good to go. They'll make a good leader because they're *already leading.*

As a leader you have to make decisions – and you have to be able to accept that you're not always going to get it right. If you get it wrong, you've got to have the mental strength to recover from that, reorganise your troops and go again. Find another solution.

AS A LEADER YOU HAVE TO MAKE DECISIONS – AND YOU HAVE TO BE ABLE TO ACCEPT THAT YOU'RE NOT ALWAYS GOING TO GET IT RIGHT.

I look round at today's world and see a lot of people in leadership positions who can't make a decision. Sometimes that's down to a lack of confidence. They don't trust themselves; they worry that they'll make the wrong call. But it's also down to team ethos. If you're a good leader then you'll have good followship, and if you've got good followship you'll create a positive ethos. Your people will go to hell and back with you, even when you get it wrong.

If you want to become a leader in your workplace or your sports team, focus your energies first on being a leader in your own life. Put in the work now, and you won't be fazed when you take on that leadership role.

ALEXANDER THE GREAT REFUSES WATER

In 325 BC, Alexander and his men set off through the desert of Gedrosia towards the royal capital. The route would take them inland, through some of the most inhospitable country imaginable, a physically shattering march lasting sixty days. According to the sources, Alexander had selected the route because he had been told that no army had ever successfully crossed it before. If that's true, this was a needlessly reckless decision and a costly one. Perhaps a third of his men would die in the Gedrosian desert, equivalent to around 12,000 soldiers.

The men suffered from constant, agonising thirst during the march. There was hardly any water to be found. Pack animals collapsed and died, too exhausted to go on. The soldiers covered extremely long distances at night and rested up during the day, but even so they became very weak. Some had to be left behind, too sick or exhausted to keep up with the punishing pace of the march. A few tried to follow their pals' tracks when they recovered their strength. The rest perished beneath the relentless desert sun.

At one point on the journey, the army was struggling through the desert in the suffocating heat of the day, having failed to find any water during the march. Alexander had insisted on leading his men on foot rather than horseback to set an example. He was badly dehydrated, his body was wracked with pain – he had every excuse for riding on horseback. But he knew the value of morale in showing his men that he was sharing in their hardship.

During the march some of the soldiers went off in search of water. All they could find was a small pool of water collected in a shallow cleft. The soldiers quickly set about gathering this water and hurried back to the army. They poured the water into a helmet and offered it to Alexander.

Alexander thanked the men, took the helmet full of water and then, in front of everyone, proceeded to pour it onto the parched ground.

Without saying a word, Alexander had communicated a powerful message to his men. *We're in this situation together,* he was saying. *And we're going to get out of it together.*

When the Macedonian soldiers saw their king tipping away the water, that gave their spirits a monumental boost. They knew they had a leader who wouldn't abandon them. He wouldn't ask them to do anything that he wouldn't do himself. They would stick together, no matter what.

By refusing to drink, Alexander was leading by example. In doing so he showed himself to be not just a great military commander: he also had a brilliant understanding of human psychology.

LESSON 51

TAKE PERSONAL RESPONSIBILITY

The military mindset places huge emphasis on personal responsibility.

At our level, you're expected to take care of your stuff. It's taken for granted that you're going to put in the work on the ranges, you're going to turn up and do your PT for a couple of hours each morning, you're going to be on top of your personal admin. When you show up for work, you're expected to be in tip-top shape, ready to go.

We're also expected to take responsibility for the decisions we make. That's a massive part of any high-performance team: taking personal responsibility when things go wrong. Admitting that it was your fault.

We're not interested in playing the blame game. We haven't got the time to mess around blaming each other. We don't necessarily care that you've made a mistake. What we really want to know is *why* the mistake happened in the first place. Where you went wrong. How we can move on from it, rectify it so that it won't happen again.

Maybe you failed to provide covering fire when we breached a compound. Why didn't you fire? Because you had suffered a stoppage with your weapon. So let's take that mistake apart. Why did you suffer a stoppage? Because you've neglected your weapon care. You didn't clean your piece properly, didn't sort your magazines out, forgot to oil the clips. You couldn't be bothered to test-fire your weapon before we went out.

There's your problem, and your solution. Admitting to the mistake, taking personal responsibility, means we can eradicate or reduce the chances of something going wrong.

But that relies on you fronting up. Owning your mistakes.

If you spend time messing around, trying to figure out where you went wrong, and you knew the answer the whole time, the military will come down hard on you.

On a good team, when everyone holds themselves accountable and admits to their mistakes, you go through what's happened, fix it and move forward. You want to go back into the fold. Good teams don't exclude people because they've made a mistake.

No one wants to screw up. No one wants to get things wrong, but it happens all the time, to all of us. The important thing is to get to the solution as fast and efficiently as possible, and that means embracing the concept of personal responsibility. Sticking your hand up. Owning your mistakes so we can find out where it went wrong.

Responsibility only works when you have a good team. It comes down to how your muckers react – and how you react to the situation at hand.

It's about saying to your mate or colleague, 'Actually, it wasn't your fault. I could have done better.'

If you're honest and open with the people in your team at work, if you're prepared to be personally responsible and learn from your mistakes, you'll have the skills to work around almost any problem.

'This, then, was the Bushido teaching – bear and face all calamities and adversities with patience and a pure conscience; for, as Mencius taught, "When Heaven is about to confer a great office on anyone, it first exercises his mind with suffering and his sinews and bones with toil; it exposes his body to hunger and subjects him to extreme poverty; and it confounds his undertakings. In all these ways it stimulates his mind, hardens his nature, and supplies his incompetencies."'

Inazo Nitobe, The Way of the Samurai

LESSON 52

BE EACH OTHER'S LIFELINE

People often ask me, 'What makes a good team?'

There's a common misconception, particularly when we're talking about elite operators, that teamwork means being dedicated and committed to the cause. But that's not really true. In any team, dedication and commitment to the cause should already be a given. It's not an added extra. I'd like to think that if you're being posted to a combat zone with a weapon in your hands, that you're absolutely dedicated and committed. That shouldn't even be up for debate.

Whether it's in the military, or in a company or institution, you should be passionate about what you do. If you treat your job like a stocking filler, as something optional in your life, then you're probably in the wrong line of work. You're never going to reach your optimum level of performance, because your head's not in the game. You're going to be on autopilot. That's actually selfish, because you're stopping your colleagues, the ones who are dedicated and committed to the cause or project, from achieving their goals, from getting to the next level – because that can only be done together. You're the weak link.

I was obsessed with soldiering. That was important, I felt, because we were playing for high stakes. If you're not totally dedicated and committed to the job, get off my team. I don't want to be anywhere near you.

What makes a good team is unconditional dedication and commitment to *each other*. That commitment is a core component of all successful teams, in every walk of life. It's indispensable. When you have that, the mission, the business project or goal you're aiming for will be within reach. Without that, you'll have a team whose members will fail to get the best out of one another.

Dedication and commitment to each other means always having the team's best interests at heart. I know what I need to do in a contact, I know my drills and skills. I know how to take down a compound, how to operate on the battlefield. But if I can get the best out of my muckers as well, if I can make them perform two or three per cent better during the mission, and I'm doing that for an eight-man team, then I'm increasing our performance by an extra sixteen or twenty-four per cent.

That's the power of being completely dedicated and committed to each other. It's about putting personal motivations aside and doing whatever is necessary to enhance the team's overall performance – adding percentages to your teammates, instead of taking them away.

Those tiny percentages can make the difference between victory and defeat on the battlefield. A good team player knows this: they won't do anything that might degrade the performance of their teammates. On the battlefield, there's no place for shouting at your pal when they make a mistake. All that does is chip away at the other person's percentages. If a high-performing soldier screws up, trust me, they're going to know about it, because they're used to operating to a very high standard. That person will be giving themselves a hard time, beating themselves up. They don't need me to come along and give them a tongue lashing, even though it would be super-easy for me to do that.

As soon as you begin the mission, whatever it may be, you have to revert to professionalism.

When someone screws up, always put the interests of the team first. Make it your priority to get their head back in the game. That sometimes means taking unpopular decisions. It might be that your colleagues react badly to someone making a mistake. It doesn't matter. It's still up to you, as the leader, to seek to maximise your team's performance. You don't want one of your teammates feeling sorry for themselves and thinking, 'You idiot, you messed up, this is all your fault.'

This approach is absolutely crucial in the military. If I'm leading a team, and one of the guys isn't fully focused on the job, that could result in someone getting shot or killed. Even if you're inwardly fuming at them, you can't afford to have their mind elsewhere, running over the mistake they've made. Any number of things could go wrong. A soldier is no use to me with his thumb up his arse. I need everyone on my team fully switched on. Therefore you need to put your feelings to one side and concentrate on restoring their focus.

Of course, after the mission or task has been completed, it's a different story. Then it is necessary to be honest with your colleagues about where they went wrong. Pinpoint the root cause of the problem: the how and why. Congratulate them on getting their heads back in the game, make sure they're not dwelling on their mistakes, because that's counter-productive – but point out where they need to improve their performance next time round.

This is a major part of teamwork. You have to know when the time is right to call people out. When to criticise them, and when you need to pick them up off the floor. That depends on the individual, their character, and the situation at the time. During training, for example, you can have a go at some-one, because it's not life and death. But if we're at a critical moment in the mission, and I come along and start shouting at one of my muckers, what does that achieve? I'm only taking away three or four per cent of that person's ability to operate.

There is a time and a place to call someone out for messing up: once you've returned from the battlefield. That's one of the reasons we have debriefs. So you can turn to your mate, look him in the eye, and tell him where he went wrong.

When you're in the heat of a firefight with the enemy, you need to have *unconditional dedication and commitment to one another*. If someone makes a mistake, I'll try to bring them back from the dead. Give them back percentages, rather than take more away. It might be something as simple as lift-ing their spirits. Telling my mate not to worry about what just happened. To keep their head up. Let them know we're in this together.

By doing this, I'm dragging my pal out of their headspace. I might be spitting mad in my head and thinking 'Jesus, I've just had to dive behind cover because you missed the target and nearly got me killed,' but I won't say anything at the time, because it's going to have a detrimental effect on my mate, and by extension the rest of the team. That two or three per cent drop in performance levels could be the difference between success and failure.

On missions, professionalism always took over. 'I'm your lifeline. You're mine.' That was our mindset. If there was a problem, we'd deal with it later at the post-op debrief. But never on the battlefield.

This is just as important in team sports, or in the workplace – wherever it may be, the same rule applies. Don't do anything that might impact negatively on your team's ability to get the job done.

People often don't realise this, but emotional and psychological connections are a fundamental aspect of teamwork. It's not just about pulling in the same direction: it's about being able to pick someone up when they've made a mistake. It's about knowing that you need to stay calm and collected in the combat zone, rather than ripping into that person and reminding them of their failure. I like to compare it to retrieving someone who's fallen into a freezing body of water. You're not going to save their life by standing there and telling them they should have been more careful. The priority is to get them out before they drown or develop hypothermia. With every passing moment, the longer they're distracted, the more their performance degrades. It's absolutely vital that you rescue them as swiftly as possible.

327

Be each other's lifeline. If a colleague is in difficulty, pull them out of the water. Then get them back in the game. Get them refocused on the mission or the task at hand.

Ignore the mistake. You can always deal with that later. Concentrate on the job. Do that, and your team will always give their maximum, no matter what.

'When someone asked why they visited disgrace upon those among them who lost their shields but did not do the same thing to those who lost their helmets or their breastplates, he said, "Because these they put on for their own sake, but the shield for the common good of the whole line."'

Demaratus, Spartan king (circa 510–491 BC)

- Build trust and teamwork through effective communication. When the people on your team learn to speaking communicate openly and honestly with one another, without even speaking, you'll create an unstoppable team.

- Cultivate and develop a shared ethos in your team. Get everyone singing off the same hymn sheet. A team that is dedicated and committed to each other will always perform to a high standard.

- Remember that good leadership means having good followship. Empower the people on your team by bringing them into the decision-making process. Leave your ego at the door. Invest in your team members, and they'll go through walls for you.

- Before you begin a task, make sure that you completely understand your role and those of your colleagues. If you don't understand something, put your hand up. Have the courage to ask questions.

- Build a consistent team through knowing your teammates inside out. A good leader will be able to spot the disconnects. When percentage points are taken away from someone's performance, work to give them back. The team will only benefit.

- Look out for one another. Get everyone pulling in the same direction. Remember: the mission doesn't always come first.

- Practise being a leader in your own life. Organise your physical and mental spaces. Stay switched on and keep your head in the game. Consistent discipline is the cornerstone of leadership.

- Embrace personal responsibility in your team. Don't exclude someone because they've screwed up. Be honest and open with each other, learn from your mistakes and move forward together.

- When your colleague or teammate is in trouble, help them out by getting their head back in the game. Be each other's lifeline.

GLOSSARY

CI – Combat Indicator

DS – Directing Staff

Duff – Royal Navy slang for dessert

DZ – Drop Zone

EP – Extraction Point

ERV – Emergency Rendezvous

FAC – Forward Air Controller

FOB – Forward Operating Base

GPMG – General Purpose Machine Gun

HLS – Helicopter Landing Site

IED – Improvised Explosive Device

IMF – Initial Military Fitness (Royal Marines)

LLP – Low-Level Parachute

LUP – Lying-Up Point

NVG – Night-Vision Goggles

PTI – Physical Training Instructor

RTU – Returned to Unit

SAS – Special Air Service

SBS – Special Boat Service

SSE – Site-Sensitive Equipment

TL – Team Leader

VI – Vehicle Interdiction

NOTE ON QUOTATIONS

For Sun Tzu's *The Art of War* I have relied on the 1910 translation from the Chinese by Lionel Giles (1876–1958), available at https://classics.mit.edu/Tzu/artwar.html.

Quotations from Niccolò Machiavelli's *The Prince* are based on the translation by William K. Marriott (1847–1927), freely available at https://www.gutenberg.org/files/1232/1232-h/1232-h.htm.

The translation of General Carl von Clausewitz's *On War* by J. Graham (1808–83) is in the public domain and available at: https://www.gutenberg.org/files/1946/1946-h/1946-h.htm.

For Epictetus's *Discourses* I have used the Thomas Wentworth Higginson (1823–1911) translation, published by Thomas Nelson and Sons in New York in 1890 as *The Works of Epictetus*, and available at the Perseus Digital Library: http://www.perseus.tufts.edu/hopper/text?doc=Perseus%3At ext%3A1999.01.0237%3Atext%3Ddisc.

The quotations from *Meditations* by Marcus Aurelius are based on the translation by George W. Chrystal (1880–1944), available at: https://www.gutenberg.org/cache/epub/55317/ pg55317-images.html.

The quote attributed to Demaratus is from the 1931 translation of Plutarch's *Sayings of Spartans* by F. C. Babbitt (1867–1935) and published in Volume III of *Moralia* (Loeb Classical Editions).

SOURCES

Abdy, Richard, *Legion: Life in the Roman Army* (The British Museum Press, 2024)

Adcock, F. E., *The Greek and Macedonian Art of War* (University of California Press, 1957)

Arrian, *Anabasis*, translated by Edward James Chinnock (Hodder & Stoughton, 1893)

Bédoyère, Guy de la, *Defying Rome* (The History Press, 2003)

Bédoyère, Guy de la, *Gladius* (Little, Brown, 2020)

Cartledge, Paul, *The Spartans* (Pan Books, 2003)

Connolly, Peter, *Greece and Rome at War* (Frontline Books, 2012)

Currey, Cecil B., *Victory at Any Cost* (Potomac Books, 2005)

Fall, Bernard, *Hell in a Very Small Place* (Da Capo Press, 2002)

Farrar-Hockley, Anthony, *The Edge of the Sword* (Pen & Sword Military, 2007)

Frere, Shepherd, *Britannia* (Cardinal, 1974)

Gabriel, Richard, *Genghis Khan's Greatest General: Subotai the Valiant* (University of Oklahoma Press, 2004)

Green, David, *Captured at the Imjin River* (Pen & Sword, 2011)

Julius Caesar, *The Gallic War*, translated by W. A. MacDevitt and W. S. Bohn (Harper & Brothers, 1869)

Kershaw, Stephen, *Barbarians* (Robinson, 2020)

Large, Lofty, *Soldier Against the Odds* (Mainstream Publishing, 1999)

Livy, *The History of Rome: The First Eight Books*, translated by D. Spillan (1853)

Livy, *The History of Rome: Books Nine to Twenty-Six*, translated by D. Spillan and Cyrus Edmonds (1868)

335

Man, John, *The Mongol Empire* (Corgi Books, 2014)

Mattingly, David, *An Imperial Possession* (Allen Lane, 2006)

Morgan, David, *The Mongols* (John Wiley & Sons, 2007)

Morris, Donald R., *The Washing of the Spears* (Pimlico, 1994)

Nepos, Cornelius, *Lives of the Eminent Commanders*, translated by John Selby Watson (1886)

Nicolle, David, *The Mongol Warlords* (Brockhampton Press, 1998)

Plutarch, *Parallel Lives*, translated by Bernadotte Perrin (Loeb Classical Library, 1901–12)

Polybius, *The Histories*, translated by W. R. Paton (Loeb Classical Library, 1922)

Ritter, E. A., *Shaka Zulu* (Penguin, 1978)

Simpson, Howard, *Dien Bien Phu* (Potomac Books, 2005)

Turnbull, Stephen, *Genghis Khan & the Mongol Conquests* (Routledge, 2003)

Xenophon, *Anabasis*, translated by Carleton L. Brownson (Heinemann, 1922)